GW00467928

equity
release
made easy

Tish Hanifan

The publisher would like to say a particular thank you to Jon King and also to Jane Finnerty for their valuable help in reviewing this book.

Published in 2008 by Age Concern Books

1268 London Road, London SW16 4ER, United Kingdom

ISBN: 978 0 86242 433 6

A catalogue record for this book is available from the British Library.

Cover design by Vincent McEvoy

Designed and typeset by Design and Media Solutions, Maidstone

Printed and bound in Great Britain by Bell & Bain Ltd, Glasgow

Contents

Introduction

Who wrote this book?

Tish Hanifan is a barrister and solicitor who specialises in older client law and is a member of Solicitors for the Elderly. She has also written many other books, including *The Solicitor's Guide to Equity Release*.

Why read it?

Like many people, you might feel let down by the worry-free retirement income promised by your pension plan and be looking for other ways of funding your life after work. You may want some extra money to pay for improvements and repairs to your home, a holiday or a car. Whatever the reason for wanting to increase your income, if you're a homeowner, one way of doing this could be to take out an equity release scheme which allows you to unlock the financial value of your home without having to move.

Equity release is only one of the options available though. It is a long-term agreement and not one to be entered into lightly – there are a number of things you need to consider carefully before deciding that it is the right choice for you.

What does it cover?

This book gives you an introduction to what can be a confusing and daunting process. It explains what equity release is, how it works, what the long-term implications of taking equity release are, what other alternatives are available, what sort of legal and financial advice you should be seeking, and where to find it. It also includes a glossary, explaining exactly what the terms used mean.

A word of warning!

Once you have signed up for an equity release scheme it may be difficult, expensive or even impossible to get out of if your circumstances change. Consider all the options available to you and always get independent financial and legal advice.

1

Your Home as an Asset

We are known in Britain as being a nation of homeowners and in recent years for many people their homes have become a valuable asset. Indeed, older people have property worth in excess of £775 billion.

However, we think of where we live not just as a financially valuable asset but as a home. It is more than just the value of the bricks and mortar – it represents both security and a haven. We feel differently about our home than about other assets we might own and certainly don't regard it in the same way as shares or ISAs.

Despite the recent slow-down in the housing market it has, nevertheless, been hard not to notice the enormous rise in the value of this asset in recent years. Figures from the Land Registry show that in 1997 the average terraced house in England was worth £52,288 and the average semi-detached £61,359. The average price in 2007 for a terraced house had risen to £141,548 and the average semi-detached to £169,150. Although this trend may not continue in the future, the effect of the years of high house price increases has often been to widen the gap between our disposable income and the amount we actually own.

So, not only does the home fulfil a psychological and emotional need, but it also represents a sound investment. It may indeed be the best investment you have ever made – many older people have not seen other financial aspects of their life perform nearly so well. Pensions, whether state or private, have not necessarily provided the worry-free income that many expected. As a consequence, people often find themselves in the frustrating position of having a more limited income in retirement than they anticipated and yet living in a property which has grown enormously in value and is their most valuable asset.

In your retirement years it could be that you would like to be able to use some of the equity (value) 'locked' in your home to provide you with the finances to enable you to do all that you have planned to do. Perhaps you would like to spend the money on improving your lifestyle, buying a new car, going on a dream holiday or paying for essential repairs or alterations to your home to make it more comfortable or practical. It might be that you would like to help your children financially while you are able to see them enjoy it. Your home could potentially be a source of additional regular income to help supplement your pension. There are ways in which you can do these things and still continue to live in your home, through methods such as equity release.

This book aims to provide you with the necessary information to help you understand all the options available to you. It will consider the different ways in which to release some equity from your home. It will guide you through the benefits and also the

potential pitfalls of the different options available –
from simply downsizing to taking out one of the
commercial equity release solutions currently on
the market.

What is equity release?

Equity release is a way of unlocking the value of
a property, without having to move home. It is
used mostly by older homeowners who either
have paid off their mortgage altogether, or have
only a small amount left to pay. As we have
already said, all the schemes are intended to be
long-term arrangements and are therefore not to
be entered into lightly. Once you have signed up
for them it may be difficult, expensive or even
impossible to get out of if your circumstances
change.

Some of the options will require that you give up
ownership of your home either completely or in
part; others that a mortgage is put on your
property. After years of saving to pay off the
mortgage this may be a difficult thing to do. If you
do decide to take this route, it will be important for
your peace of mind to understand fully what this
will mean in terms of your rights and security of
tenure – in other words, your right to remain in the
home for your lifetime. These will be set out in the
terms and conditions of the lender's offer to you. If
you are not happy to accept them, then equity
release may not be for you.

If you do decide to go ahead and make use of the
value of your home to provide additional income

or capital, then it is important to remember this will inevitably have an effect upon any inheritance you might wish to leave to your family.

Most of the schemes for equity release work either by 'selling' a part of your home ('home reversion plans': see Chapter 4) or by taking out a mortgage in which the interest is 'rolled up' until death ('lifetime mortgages': see Chapter 3). Remember that either of these methods will result in a loss of assets to pass on after your death. It is for this reason that you might consider discussing the possibilities with your family – it may be that they can help in some way. We consider this in more detail in Chapter 2.

Equity release schemes are not right for everybody and Age Concern recommends that you **always get independent legal and financial advice** before taking out an equity release plan. You will be able to get advice from financial advisers who specialise in this area and also from your solicitor who will explain the legal aspects involved and help you understand the terms and conditions of any contract. How to find legal and financial advice is explored in more detail in Chapter 6. Chapter 7 lists further sources of help.

As these are long-term arrangements, you have to be particularly careful to take into account what may happen in the future. Your circumstances may change as you get older and it is important to have considered how any course of action taken now might affect your future options, such as possibly having to fund care. So Chapter 5 considers what effect your decisions now might have later in life.

This book is intended to give you an independent view of all the options available so that you can begin to decide what is right for you. It highlights both the advantages and disadvantages of the different schemes and helps you to avoid the pitfalls by looking at what could go wrong. It is not a substitute for good advice from a financial adviser or solicitor about your particular circumstances but is intended as a guide to help you understand more about the options for taking money from the value of your home. These schemes have been around for quite a while now and providers in the market have developed a wide range of products, with new ideas frequently coming onto the market, so it is important to take advice from someone who knows about the whole range of options.

History of equity release

The first reversion income scheme was introduced in 1965, by Home Reversions (later named Hodge Equity Release).This was followed in 1972 by the first home income plan based on a mortgage and an annuity. (An annuity is a financial product purchased from an insurance company that converts a lump sum into a regular income and is taxed.)

Lenders in this market began to develop a range of products to meet the need for people to use some of the money tied up in their homes without having to move. In 1988 some unsafe schemes, including investment bond schemes and 'roll-up plans' with variable interest rates, began to appear. These left many older people in financial difficulties, and so the City regulators took action to stop them being sold. The recognition by the providers of the plans that there were these potential problems led to the formation in 1991 of Safe Home Income Plans (SHIP) which was established to promote only the safe schemes.

SHIP (see address in Chapter 7) is supported by many of the providers in the equity release market. All participating companies have to observe the SHIP Code of Conduct which requires member companies to provide a fair, easy-to-understand and full presentation of their plans. All SHIP members insist that independent legal advice is taken and will only accept applications from specifically qualified advisers. All members display the SHIP logo in their brochures and other printed material as a guarantee to customers. Importantly, all SHIP plans carry a 'no negative equity' guarantee – this means that you will never owe more than the value of your home. They also guarantee that people can move from their property with any financial penalty (this is explored further in Chapters 3 and 4). Protection for the consumer has also been strengthened by the Financial Services Authority (FSA) regulating both lifetime mortgages and home reversions. This is explained in more detail in Chapter 6.

Before we look at some of the current schemes in more detail, we must say again – these schemes are intended to be long-term arrangements and may therefore be difficult to get out of if you reconsider or if your circumstances change. Some of the options will have a direct effect upon your ownership, as home reversion plans require you to sell all or part of your home to the reversion company. Remember too that equity release will also affect your plans to leave an inheritance.

2

Before You Begin

If you are looking to increase your income or capital in retirement, or to adapt your home so you can continue to live there, it is important to remember that equity release is just one of the options available.

In this chapter we look at some of the things you should consider before deciding to pursue the various forms of equity release. In particular, we consider what other options might be open to you.

Downsizing

Many people decide that retirement is a time to make significant changes to their lives and in doing so consider moving house. This may be to bring about a lifestyle change or it may be that the home is now too big if children have moved out. You may feel it makes no financial sense to be rattling around in a property which is too big for your needs as well as being increasing costly and time-consuming to maintain.

Downsizing (in other words, moving to a smaller, less expensive property) may provide both a useful lump sum for you to spend as you choose and significantly reduce your household expenditure.

If you are considering downsizing, it is very important to be clear why you are moving and what you want to achieve by doing so. If the house is too big and you are looking to move because of the convenience of a new smaller or perhaps purpose-built house, this will not necessarily cost you any less to buy than the value of your current home. It will partly depend on the area to which you wish to move. Some areas popular for retirement have house prices that are above the national average.

Bear in mind that if you may buy a smaller home, it won't necessarily cost you less to maintain. For example if the property you are moving to is on a development with some enhanced services, such as communal gardens, cleaners or maintenance people, then there may well be service charges which will eat into the additional income produced by reducing the outgoings on your previous larger home.

There are also significant costs associated with selling and buying property – for example, you will have to pay your estate agent and solicitor as well as removal costs. If the home you buy is worth more than £125,000, you will also have to pay Stamp Duty. Currently this is:

- 1% on properties £125,001 to £250,000
- 3% on properties between £250,001 and £500,000
- 4% on properties over £500,000.

The costs may not just be financial, as moving home can be a very stressful experience. Downsizing may require you to part with items that you have accumulated over the years and which you have an emotional attachment to. It could also mean moving away from the support of friends and neighbours.

Family arrangements

Involving your family in your financial affairs is not for everyone. It may be that you don't want to discuss your finances with your children and their partners and certainly don't want to be a financial burden to them. This is entirely your decision and you should never feel pressurised to involve them if this is not something you feel comfortable doing. However, it might be that you have an open relationship with your children with regard to financial matters and you would be happy to discuss your plans with them. Your children may prefer to help you financially rather than you involve an equity release company.

If a member of your family would prefer that you borrowed money from them rather than enter into a commercial arrangement, then it is essential that both parties receive independent legal advice. With the best intentions in the world, arrangements with family members can go wrong and it will cause fewer problems in the long term if both parties are clear about the terms which affect them. The terms agreed between you both should be put into writing. This should include important points such as:

- whether there is any interest to pay
- if so, when it will be due?
- how, if at all, the loan will be secured – for example, will there be a charge against the property (a mortgage)?
- in what circumstances the money will be repayable – for example, on the death of one of the parties or if you move into a care home.

A solicitor will advise you on all these aspects. They will also explain some of the possible pitfalls, such as:

- The family member lending the money is married and subsequently **divorces**: the loan would be considered to be part of the marital assets and might have to be repaid
- The family member lending the money **dies**: the loan would be an asset of their estate and the executor would have to account for this to the beneficiaries
- The family member lending the money becomes **bankrupt**: the loan is an asset which passes to the creditors.

All these matters should be considered and discussed so that a clear written agreement can be produced which reflects the wishes and intentions of both parties. It would also be a good idea for both the parties to review their wills at this point.

Remember, although your children might welcome the opportunity to provide the lump sum you need to release from the equity in your home rather than you incurring the charges involved in a scheme, this may have implications both for your own tax situation and for your children's. In particular, if you give part of your home to your children in return for a lump sum you may become liable to a relatively new tax called 'pre-owned assets' tax. It is essential that before going ahead you take advice.

Grants and loans

If you are considering taking out an equity release plan because you want to make any repairs or improvements to your property, it is worth considering whether there might be any grants or loans available to help with this work before going ahead with equity release.

Below is a summary of some of the grants and loans that might be available to you.

Disabled Facilities Grants

These grants are available to provide facilities and adaptations to help a disabled person to live as independently and in as much comfort as possible.

Am I eligible?

You will be considered a 'disabled person' for the purposes of this grant if:

- your sight, hearing or speech is substantially impaired
- you have a mental disorder or impairment of any kind
- you are physically substantially disabled by illness or injury (the impairment may have been present since birth or may have occurred at a later date).

To apply for this grant you can either be the owner or the tenant of the property. Another person can make an application on your behalf if you are a disabled person requiring the works. The applicant will need to provide the council with a certificate stating that you, the disabled occupant, will live in the property for at least five years after the works are completed.

Mr and Mrs Smith live in a terraced house which they jointly purchased under the Right to Buy scheme 10 years ago. Mrs Smith has developed Motor Neurone Disease and Mr Smith needs to adapt the house to include a downstairs shower room. He also wants to make the downstairs area open plan, widen the doors and put in ramps so that Mrs Smith's wheelchair can be used more easily. Mr Smith can make the application on behalf of his wife.

Other types of work covered by this grant include:

- stairlifts
- safety improvements, such as improved lighting
- adapting existing facilities – such as the controls for heating and lighting – to make them easier to use
- kitchen and bathroom facilities
- improving the heating system (a disabled person may need extra heating if they are less mobile).

How do I apply?

Disabled facilities grants are made by local Housing Departments and you need to make your application to them before any work starts or you will not be entitled to any financial help. You can start by asking either your local Housing Department or the local Social Services Department about applying for a grant.

Although the Housing Department will decide whether to make the grant, it will consult with

Social Services to decide whether the adaptations are 'necessary and appropriate'. In order for the local authority to decide this you will usually have a visit from an occupational therapist to assess the kind of help they consider the disabled person needs. The Housing Department also has to be sure the work is reasonable – not just appropriate to the needs of the disabled person but also with consideration to the age and condition of the property. To do this it will usually send either an Environmental Health Officer or a surveyor to look at the property. Sometimes it sends someone from the Home Improvement Agency (see page 17).

How much financial assistance is available?

This means tested grant applies to disabled people and their spouse or civil partner. It doesn't take any account of the means of the actual owner of the property if this is a different person from the disabled applicant.

Mrs Patel is on a low income and in receipt of benefits. She needs to make adaptations to her bathroom and she makes an application for a Disabled Facilities Grant. The house is owned by her son who has a full-time job and is a higher-rate taxpayer – so wouldn't qualify for help as he has too much income. However, this will not affect Mrs Patel's application which will be based on her own financial position. This is the case even though her son owns the property and could therefore be said to be receiving a benefit.

The means test takes into account the average weekly income of the relevant people. Some benefits and savings up to £6,000 are ignored. This is then compared with an assessment of the applicant's basic needs. If the applicant's resources are less than this the local authority will meet all the costs (the maximum allowance as a Disabled Facilities Grant is £30,000). As this means test is complicated it is best to seek more detailed advice (see Chapter 7).

Community equipment

If you are not eligible for a Disabled Facilities Grant, or not entitled to the full amount, your local Social Services Department may be able to help you with a contribution towards the cost; known as 'top-up funding'. It is worth noting that Social Services Departments also provide 'community equipment', such as grab rails and ramps, up to a value of £1,000 if an applicant has been assessed as needing this help. These must be provided free of charge.

Warm Front Grants

This scheme provides help with heating and insulation improvements for people living in England. Grants are available to householders who are aged 60 or over and also to disabled people. To be eligible for this grant an applicant must be in receipt of a qualifying benefit such as Housing Benefit, Council Tax Benefit or Pension Credit. The Warm Front scheme is run by EAGA and you can apply for a grant by phoning 0800 3162805 (see Chapter 7 for full details of how to make contact).

If you are interested in the grant but are not
currently in receipt of a qualifying benefit, EAGA
offers a 'Benefit entitlement check' service through
Warm Front to see if you might be eligible for one of
the qualifying benefits but are not claiming it. You
can do this by phoning 0800 0729006.

There is also a scheme called 'Warm Front 300'. If
you are over 60 but are not eligible for a Warm
Front Grant, there is a one-off non-means-tested
grant of £300 towards the cost of a new boiler.

If you live in Wales, of 60 or over and receive an
income-related benefit, you may be eligible to
receive a grant from The Home Energy Efficiency
Scheme (HEES Wales) – to find out phone 0800
316 2815. If you live in Scotland and are in receipt
of income related benefits you ma be entitled to a
grant from the Warm Deal scheme. For more
information phone Scottish Gas (which runs the
programme on behalf of the Scottish Government)
on 0800 316 1653 or 6009.

Other sources of finance

Charities

Many charities have grants or funds available
which may help you to improve your home or to
carry out necessary maintenance. The criteria for
eligibility varies depending on the individual
charity. Age Concern has a helpful factsheet on
this (see Chapter 7).

The Social Fund

You may be entitled to a Community Care Grant or

a Budgeting Loan from the Social Fund for help towards the cost of minor repairs or essential decoration.

To apply for this you will need to be in receipt of State Pension. The payments are discretionary and the Social Fund budget is limited; staff at your local Social Security office will decide whether you can have a grant or loan. For further information, contact your local Social Security office.

Other ways of getting help to stay at home

Home Improvement Agencies

These are not-for-profit organisations that are locally managed by councils, charities or housing associations. They are sometimes called 'Care and Repair' or 'Staying Put'. They provide support for vulnerable people to help them to carry out adaptations, repairs and improvements to their home. Help is offered on how to access financial support for the work that needs to be done as well as technical support in the planning of the work. They will also ensure the work is undertaken by an accredited tradesman.

Many Home Improvement Agencies (HIAs) also offer housing-based services to enable vulnerable people to retain as much independence as possible in their own home. This could be help with security or energy efficiency improvements, or routine services such as gardening and decorating. The national body which coordinates all the HIAs is called Foundations (see Chapter 7 for details of how to contact them).

Home Improvement Trust

If you want to raise capital from your home specifically to pay for repairs, improvements or adaptations, the Home Improvement Trust (HIT) may be able to help. HIT is a not-for-profit organisation set up in 1997 with the support of what is now the Department for Communities and Local Government. Its aim is to enable older homeowners and those with a disabled person in their household to live safely and independently in the home.

The Trust has set up and operates the 'Houseproud' scheme to help older homeowners release some of the equity tied up in their home, in order to fund repairs, improvements or adaptations. The programme gives practical help and advice on repairs, improvements and adaptations. It also helps to source reliable tradespeople and checks the work on completion.

Here are some examples of the kind of work you can get help with:
- new bathroom
- electrical rewiring
- central heating
- new roof
- replacement windows and doors
- new guttering

- plumbing
- refitted kitchen
- improved home security
- disabled adaptations, such as a level-access shower
- improving your home's energy efficiency.

HIT also provides information on funding options, including 'no-risk equity release loans', and has links with lenders who provide low-cost loans to older people with the money raised against the value of their homes. The lenders are regulated banks or building societies who provide a written guarantee of no repossession while the original borrower remains in occupation. As with all equity release plans, the terms of the loan offered will depend upon the lender and it is important to seek financial advice if you are considering this option.

Rent a Room scheme

If you have a spare room and would consider having somebody sharing your home, then the 'Rent a Room' scheme might be a way to obtain some additional income. It allows you to receive a certain amount of tax-free income from renting furnished accommodation in your only or main home. Currently the amount is £4,250 a year. You can choose to take advantage of the scheme if you let furnished accommodation in the home where you live to a lodger. A lodger is someone who pays to live in your home and also shares use of the family rooms.

If you decide to take in a lodger, and you have a mortgage, it's important to contact

your lender and check whether taking in a lodger is allowed within its terms and conditions. Usually the lender will just want to be told about your plans but occasionally it may require you to have additional insurance. You should also check to see what additional health and safety requirements there might be; for example you might need to provide smoke alarms. Your local authority Housing Department will be able advise you on this. This scheme could be both a very useful way to earn some extra income and at the same time provide a degree of company.

It is essential that you make very careful background checks on anyone who is going to live in your home. Always take up references and ensure that you have proof of identity (such as driving licence or passport). Arrange for someone to be with you when a potential lodger comes to view and do not discuss your personal arrangements or routines. When advertising for a lodger you can specify whether you wish to let to a male or female (this is an exception to the sex discrimination legislation).

It is not legally necessary to have a written agreement but is advisable to do so. Such an agreement should include references to:

- how long the letting will last
- the amount of rent to be paid and when it falls due (such as weekly or monthly)
- how much notice either party has to give in order to terminate the arrangement.

It would also be a good idea to seek legal advice about the contract. Your local Citizens Advice Bureau or the national charity Shelter may be able to help (see Chapter 7 for details of how to make contact).

Homeshare

Another way in which you might use a spare room in your house is with a scheme called Homeshare. This works with the householder offering accommodation to a homesharer in exchange for an agreed level of help. The householder may require help with household tasks or some financial support or both. Homeshare programmes aim to enable older people to remain independent in their own home by finding a homesharer willing to offer support and/or a modest income to the householder. For more information visit www.homeshare.org.uk.

Are you claiming all the benefits you are entitled to?

If your reason for considering equity release is because you are looking to supplement your current income then it is important to first find out whether you are claiming all the benefits to which you are entitled. Both your entitlement to benefits and the process of claiming them can be very complicated. This is particularly true of those benefits that are means tested and is the reason many benefits go unclaimed. In fact, although currently around one-third of all pensioners receive a means-tested benefit in some form, it is thought that approximately half of all pensioners are actually eligible to receive help. So it is very important to get some advice. Your local Age Concern or Citizens Advice Bureau may be able to help you with this. Age Concern also has a range of factsheets and guides on benefit entitlement and there is more information in the Age Concern book *Your Rights to Money Benefits*.

Making sure you are receiving all the benefits you are entitled to may mean that you don't need to proceed with equity release after all.

Already in receipt of benefits?

If you are already receiving benefits then it is important to consider whether receiving capital and/or income from an equity release scheme will affect your entitlement to any means-tested benefits, as the money you receive from the plan will improve your financial position.

There are some benefits where entitlement is not affected by the income and/or capital generated by equity release. These are non-means-tested benefits and depend on satisfying conditions relating to National Insurance contributions, disability or other non-means-tested criteria. They include Attendance Allowance, Carer's Allowance and State Retirement Pension. There is a further range of means-tested benefits which may be affected by equity release – for example entitlement to Pension Credit, Council Tax Benefit and other health benefits such as help with the cost of glasses and dental treatment.

Benefits and the effect of equity release

Benefits for those under State Pension age	
Not affected by equity release	**May be affected by equity release**
Child Benefit	Income-Based Jobseeker's Allowance (JSA)
Contribution-Based Jobseeker's Allowance (JSA)	Income Support (up to age 60)
Disability Living Allowance	Council Tax Benefit
Incapacity Benefit	Health Benefits (free prescriptions, free school meals, free milk and vitamins, free sight tests, help with the costs of glasses and dental treatment)
Carer's Allowance	

Benefits for those over State Pension age	
Not affected by equity release	**May be affected by equity release**
Attendance Allowance	Pension Credit (from age 60)
State Retirement Pension	Council Tax Benefit
Carer's Allowance	Health Benefits (help with the costs of glasses and dental treatment: other elements are free to those over 60)

Source: Council of Mortgage Lenders *Equity release and the impact on benefits and tax,* April 2008

All sums you receive from any type of equity release will be considered for benefits purposes as being either capital or income. Usually, it will be clear into which category the sum falls. A product which produces a single cash lump sum is viewed as capital. One which produces a regular amount of money in the future will be considered to be income. However, some products produce a series of lump sums or instalments. If a sum is received which puts the benefit recipient above a certain level of income or capital then benefit entitlement will cease.

> **Mr Hawkins,** who is a pensioner, qualifies for Council Tax Benefit (CTB). He receives a State Pension and receives a lump sum from an equity release scheme. If he had no capital at all, and the lump sum he acquired was only £6,000, then there would be no effect on the CTB provision (as the first £6,000 of capital is ignored). If the lump sum was larger, and took his capital above £16,000, he would lose his entitlement. If, instead, Mr Hawkins took the money he had generated from equity release as income, the receipt of the income would decrease the amount of CTB payable. This is because CTB entitlement reduces as the recipient's income rises – it wouldn't necessarily stop the applicant from being entitled altogether.

With both Pension Credit and Council Tax Benefit, where a lender is making payments at regular intervals under an equity release scheme, such amounts will be treated as income, not capital.

These are all matters that you should take into account when considering whether equity release is right for you. A financial adviser looking at equity release is required to take account of the effect on welfare benefits (see Chapter 6) and will always go through this with you before recommending any equity release solution.

One of the dangers of unregulated schemes is that they don't always consider the effect of taking out an equity scheme on your current benefit entitlement. Always check you are receiving the correct benefits.

This chapter has highlighted some of the things you should consider before beginning to look in more detail at the range of equity release options available. In particular, we have looked at the alternative options to equity release.

Once you have considered all these, it is time to find out more about what is available and how the particular plans might meet your needs. This is where it is vital to seek good advice. A limited number of companies sell their products without providing advice. These are referred to as 'non-advised' sales. Although it is legal for these companies to do so and you don't have to get advice, Age Concern strongly suggests that you do so. How to find an adviser and what you can expect them to do for you are covered in detail in Chapter 6.

In the next two chapters we will look in more detail at the two standards forms of equity release: lifetime mortgages and home reversion plans.

3

Lifetime Mortgages

What is a lifetime mortgage?

A lifetime mortgage is an equity release arrangement that is designed to help you remain in your home for as long as you wish while benefiting from the capital you have locked up in the property. You still own your home and raise money against the value of it by taking out a mortgage. The money released can be taken in a number of ways, such as a lump sum, regular withdrawals or a combination of the two.

This chapter will look at how lifetime mortgages work, how they have developed, what you need to consider and the reasons you need to take independent financial and legal advice before entering into this type of arrangement.

How does a lifetime mortgage work?

A lifetime mortgage loan is secured against the value of your property. Typically, no repayments need be made as would be the case with a normal mortgage and the interest will be added or 'rolled into' your loan, with the full amount paid back when your home is eventually sold. The proceeds of the sale are used to repay the initial loan amount plus any 'rolled-up' interest. Any equity left is returned to you or your estate.

Interest is compounded on a roll-up mortgage, so you pay interest on interest and the debt can increase quite quickly over the years. Very often, this has an effect on the percentage you can borrow against the value of your property.

Typically, at age 60 most lenders will advance only around 20% of your property's value, rising to around 50% if you are in your 80s. This will vary from lender to lender, depending on the terms of the lifetime mortgage. The valuation of your home and any outstanding debt that needs to be cleared will also influence the amount you are likely to be offered.

How you release money also affects the amounts available to you. Most schemes let you take a lump sum upfront or fixed amounts in regular instalments – some schemes allow you to take a combination of the two. It's worth noting that how you take the money – say, as a lump sum or as a monthly income – will affect how quickly the amount of mortgage debt rolls up. We look at this further later in the chapter.

Is a lifetime mortgage right for you?

Most lenders will insist on a minimum amount borrowed, so if you only want to borrow a small amount (for essential house repairs, for example), then the costs of taking out an equity release plan might not make this the most cost-effective option (see Chapter 2 for alternatives).

Using the money to invest is something that an adviser would recommend you consider very carefully as, when the costs of a scheme are considered, it is unlikely that your investment would perform well enough to make it worth your while. However, many people, with good advice and planning, can, and do, use lifetime mortgages as a way of providing extra retirement income. The money can be spent on whatever you like, although the amount you decide to release needs serious thought – **equity release can affect your entitlement to means-tested benefits, so you should always check this with an independent financial adviser**. This is covered in more detail in Chapter 2.

Most lifetime mortgages have similar features, terms and conditions but, increasingly, competition means that each lender is offering their own unique features. However, no matter which lender you use there are some important considerations you need to bear in mind.

You need to ask yourself what your needs are likely to be over the next few years and whether the scheme you are considering will allow further release of funds in the future. How will the scheme you choose impact on your choices if you need to move into a care home, for example, or want to fund care at home? Having access to lump sums of cash held as savings or as regular income from a lifetime mortgage could affect the amount and type of help you may receive to fund you or your partner's care. You should take advice to help you think your options through. These considerations are covered fully in Chapter 5.

The term 'lifetime' suggests that the arrangement is for the whole of your life but, in fact, with some schemes there is flexibility as to how long the arrangement lasts. Remember, though, that all schemes are intended to be long-term arrangements. Indeed, there may be financial penalties to pay ('redemption penalties') if the arrangement is ended for reasons other than those agreed in the contract. If you move house and if the lender allows, you may be able to transfer the loan to the new property rather than start a new arrangement. Typical reasons for the mortgage arrangement coming to an end and the loan being repaid will be when you move into long-term care or sheltered housing and in some cases just selling your home to move to another. Some schemes may limit your options to move out, so you need to consider your future plans too.

It is also worth noting that if there is no equity left when you die, your beneficiaries would have to repay any debt above the value of your home from your estate. To safeguard against this, most lifetime mortgages offer a **'no-negative-equity guarantee'**. With this guarantee, the lender promises that you (or your beneficiaries) will never have to pay back more than the value of your home – even if the debt has become larger than this. This guarantee is offered by all SHIP members.

Here is an example of the no-negative-equity guarantee:

Mrs East's home is worth £160,000. She borrowed £45,000 at a fixed rate of interest of 7%. There are no monthly payments. Interest is added on and rolled up over the lifetime of the loan. After 20 years, she owed the lender £174,136. This includes the £45,000 she originally borrowed. After death, if the house was sold for, say, £170,000, this is all that would be paid back to the lender. Mrs East's estate would not have to repay the outstanding debt.

Many lifetime mortgages are now more flexible and better adapted to customers' needs than in the past. Some can take into consideration your state of health, for example, and adapt to future plans such as the need for more money. The fact that there is so much more choice now is why you should always take the time to seek independent specialist advice. New regulations mean that if you receive advice from an authorised adviser they must take reasonable care to ensure the suitability of their advice and it will give you the opportunity to make a better informed choice as well as having added protection.

The main types of lifetime mortgages

Roll-up mortgage

'Rolled up' refers to how the interest is added to the mortgage loan. You receive a lump sum and/or a regular income on the money you receive. Interest is charged monthly or yearly, adding to the mortgage loan you originally took out. When your home is eventually sold, you will need to repay your original loan plus the interest that has rolled-up over the number of years the loan has run for.

This has been the most popular type of scheme because until relatively recently other options – such as a regular drawdown of income – were not available. When taking the loan out you are usually offered a range of interest rate options. If you are looking for complete peace of mind and want to be sure about the rate at which your loan is rolling up, then a fixed rate could be an option to consider. But, if you do take a fixed rate you will be unable to take advantages of interest rates should they fall; on the other hand you are cushioned from the risk of them rising.

Example of how interest rolled up impacts on your equity

Initial property value   £300,000
Initial loan amount   £100,000
Loan rate (fixed)   7%

Loan repaid after	Outstanding loan plus interest	Equity *(this is the value of the property after the loan and interest has been repaid)*
5 years	£140,255	£159,745
10 years	£196,715	£103,285
15 years	£275,903	£24,097

Drawdown schemes

If you are looking for greater flexibility than a lump-sum equity release could offer and you are worried about the speed at which your equity debt will accumulate, then a drawdown equity release scheme may suit you better and offer the flexibility you are looking for.

A drawdown lifetime mortgage has broadly the same advantages and disadvantages as a regular lifetime mortgage, as well as a few features specific to this kind of scheme. The main difference with a drawdown lifetime mortgage is that, instead of taking the full amount of the loan straightaway, you decide on a maximum amount of equity you want to release, and 'drawdown' the cash in stages as you require it – either at various times depending on your need or at regular intervals.

Chapter 5 explains how taking income like this may affect you in the future should you need to go into residential care.

Main benefits of a drawdown lifetime mortgage

- You can drawdown money as and when you need it, or you may be able to request a monthly income
- You only pay interest on the actual amount of equity released, so interest will accumulate more slowly than with a lump-sum lifetime mortgage
- You retain more control, as you only release equity when it suits you
- Drawdown plans can be better if you are at the younger end of the age eligibility (aged 60+).

Here is an example of a need for both cash and additional income:

Rachel and Bruce Carter are married; Rachel is the younger, aged 70. They own a property worth £250,000.

With a joint pension income in addition to their state pensions of £15,000 per year, Rachel and Bruce wish to spend some money on their home, to build a conservatory and a new kitchen. They also want some additional income, as they have investigated other options and know they are not entitled to any additional benefits such as Pension Credit.

They decide to release the £17,500 lump sum needed for their home improvements and an additional monthly 'income' of £325 using a suitable lifetime mortgage plan.

The house is improved, increasing its value and its enjoyment to Rachel and Bruce. The monthly 'income' actually comprises a series of small loan increments. This carries no income tax, and the loan grows much more slowly than if a larger lump sum is taken at the outset.

Main drawbacks of a drawdown lifetime mortgage

- The interest rates offered can sometimes be higher on a drawdown plan than on a standard lifetime mortgage

- If you want to increase the amount of equity released beyond the original you agreed, a further advance may not always be possible
- There can be restrictions on the minimum amount you can release
- Interest on a drawdown mortgage is still rolled up, as with a lump-sum scheme
- You may not be able to raise as much money through equity release with a drawdown lifetime mortgage as you may be able to with a reversion scheme, for example. (A reversion scheme is another type of equity release discussed in the next chapter)
- As with all lifetime mortgages, if you repay the loan off early you may have to pay an early repayment charge.

Fixed repayment lifetime mortgage

A fixed repayment lifetime mortgage, sometimes known as a 'discounted mortgage' scheme, is a less typical type of scheme. The reference to 'fixed' in this case is nothing to do with the interest rate you are charged but refers to the way the loan is repaid. You receive your lump sum of money but you don't have to pay any interest back. Instead, when your home is sold, you have to repay the lender a higher amount than you borrowed (this amount can sometimes be agreed in advance). The higher sum repays the mortgage when your home is sold. There are only one or two such schemes available, and whether or not it is good value depends on how long you live – in other words, the longer you live the better value it is.

Interest-only mortgage

This is very similar to a standard mortgage where the lender would require you (or perhaps your family if that was the agreement you entered into) to pay the interest on the loan. The rate can be fixed or variable. The amount you originally borrowed remains the same and is repaid when your home is eventually sold. These are usually quite flexible arrangements and, importantly, some people could benefit with help to pay the interest on this kind of arrangement.

Where the equity you release is to be used for 'essential' repairs and improvements by a homeowner and you are entitled to Pension Credit, you would be able to get an increase in your Pension Credit to cover the cost of the interest. This would provide in effect an almost interest-free lifetime mortgage.

Home income plan

With a home income plan, the money you borrow is used to buy a regular fixed income for life (usually in the form of an annuity). This income is used to pay the interest on the mortgage and whatever is left is yours to use. Unlike the other lifetime mortgages described above, the income here is not tax free. This is because it comes from an annuity and so doesn't therefore benefit from any concession. You may be taxed on this income, depending on your circumstances. The additional amount of income you receive from the plan may be enough to put you into a higher tax bracket when added to your existing income. This could mean you either begin to pay tax or you pay more tax than you did before you took out the plan. The amount you originally borrowed is repaid when your home is eventually sold. These schemes are likely to be most suitable for older people who can get higher annuity rates but it's important to note that a fixed income would be eroded by inflation over time.

Are lifetime mortgages available to everyone?

Lifetime mortgages are *not* available to everyone – a lender will usually be looking for certain criteria before they will consider you for a lifetime mortgage arrangement. These include:

- your age (or ages if you are applying as a couple: usually the age of the younger partner is the most important factor)
- the type and value of your property (some companies have a minimum value property that they will consider)
- the type and structure of the property (for example, whether is it of standard brick construction)
- whether it is a leasehold property and, if so, how long the lease is
- whether you own your home outright or only have a small mortgage or loan outstanding
- who else (if anyone) lives in your home
- with some schemes, the state of your health will also be a factor.

Your age

Your age, or combined ages, usually determines how much of your equity you can release. While some plans start as low as age 55, most require borrowers to be over 60. The younger you are, the less you can usually release, as you are likely to be rolling up your interest payments for longer. This will mean that much less equity will be left when the mortgage finally has to be repaid (and possibly none at all if the plan continues for a long time). For this reason, lifetime mortgages may not be suitable for younger ages; many plans stipulate a minimum age of 60 years.

While, in theory, you can't be too old to take out an equity release scheme, the expense involved relative to the amount you receive and the length of time you can enjoy the benefits means that if you are in your 80s you need to consider very carefully whether equity release is suitable for you (a good financial adviser would discuss this with you) or whether there are any other more suitable options (see Chapter 2).

How much of a lump sum can you get?

Your age also influences the proportion of the current value of your home you will be offered. If you are considering entering into the arrangement as a couple (if you are married or in a civil partnership and own your home as joint tenants), the relevant age is usually the younger of the partners, as you will both have a right to continue to live in the property for the rest of your lives.

As an example, typically 20% of the value can be released where the homeowner is aged 60, with this increasing by one percentage point for each year that the age is above 60. There is usually an upper limit too – typically of 45% at age 85 or 50% at age 90. Limiting the amount you can release based on age reduces the risk that the loan will roll up to be more than the value of your home.

The type and value of your property

Most lenders want to see a minimum property value of around £75,000 to £80,000. But, most equity release lenders will not lend on certain types of property. The property needs to be in good repair and of 'standard' construction (such as brick). If it is leasehold, lenders will require a minimum number of years left on the lease (typically 80 years plus).

The range of properties on which equity release is now available is wide (though typically not quite as wide as for conventional mortgage lending). However, if the property is a flat, where it is situated may be an issue and freehold flats are usually not suitable. Many lenders will not lend against high-rise flats or flats above shops. Sheltered housing may also be a problem, as will instances where you own only part of your home. These kinds of properties may not provide suitable security for some lenders. Chalet-type 'park homes' and some former local authority housing, for example, may not be acceptable either because the lender might be concerned that the property may not grow sufficiently in value over the time of the mortgage.

However, as more providers enter the market, there may be some specialist lenders who will consider a wider range of property. It is important to seek financial advice, especially if your home falls into one of the above categories, as a specialist adviser will have a detailed knowledge of all the market options. You have to be prepared to pay for a survey when applying for a lifetime mortgage and this will highlight any work needing to be carried out. The individual lender's terms and conditions should be checked before you apply, to make sure you do not go to the expense of a survey on a property the lender will not consider as security.

Existing mortgages

If you still have an existing mortgage on your property, you may be able to use part of the lifetime mortgage to repay this and any other outstanding debt secured on it. This might leave you with little left to spend but would free up income that had been used on paying the existing mortgage every month. Again, if you are receiving any benefits to help with mortgage payments, you need to consider the impact equity release could have on them too.

If the property is jointly owned both the owners must apply. The property should ideally also be held in your joint names on a joint tenancy basis rather than as tenants in common. A property held as tenants in common may be acceptable to a limited number of lenders but a lot will depend on the value of the respective shares compared with the amount you are looking to release. Even for those who will consider this form of ownership, as a general rule the amount to be borrowed should not exceed the value of the 50% share each party will own in the property.

If you are not sure how you own the property, you should contact your solicitor. It may be that you have made wills which, for tax purposes, have required that you change the usual form of ownership of joint tenants to that of tenants in common. If that is the case, then before proceeding with equity release you should seek legal and financial advice.

Mr and Mrs Baxter are both 68 and their home is valued at £600,000 with a small mortgage of £50,000. They decide they want to release 15% of their equity to cover their existing mortgage and to pay for a conservatory and redecoration of their home. The lender paid off the £50,000 to their existing lender, leaving them with £40,000 to cover the improvements to their home and the opportunity to draw down further funds if needed in the future. The Baxters have no monthly mortgage repayments now, which is a boost to their income.

Before going ahead, always check that releasing capital as a lump sum or regular income will not affect any benefits to which you may be entitled. Look at all the alternatives for funding the improvements you want and also the ability to move in the future.

Who else lives in your home?

If there are other people living with you, such as a partner you are not married to, relatives or carers, the mortgage lender is likely to ask them to sign a disclaimer giving up any rights they may have to living in the property when the equity release arrangement comes to an end. Some lenders may not allow this at all. The lender needs to ensure they can get vacant possession of the property in order to sell it and get their money back. Adults occupying the property at the time the arrangement was entered into might otherwise have acquired some rights of occupation which would either make it difficult for the lender to sell the property or would devalue it. So if, for example, you have a partner to whom you are not married and they are not party to the agreement, they may lose their home if you were to die or move out into long-term care, as the property would have to be sold and they would have signed away their rights to continue living in the property when they signed the disclaimer.

It is important to discuss this with anyone who is currently living with you and who is not an owner of the property. They should be advised to take independent advice about their legal position in the event of a sale (see Chapters 5 and 6).

The state of your health

Poor health is not a barrier to taking out equity release but it may mean you need to think about some of the other options considered in Chapter 2, for example you might qualify for benefits such as Attendance Allowance. Equity release may restrict your ability to get these benefits.

Age is a big factor in determining how much money can be released, but if your life expectancy is shortened by certain medical conditions, some lenders take this into the calculation when determining the amount of equity. These 'enhanced terms' mean that a larger amount can be released than you would otherwise have received. Should you buy an annuity with the lump sum, this too is likely to give you enhanced levels of income.

Other things to consider

How much money should I release?

Many things apart from your age and health influence how much you decide to release. Independent financial advice will help you take an objective view of your circumstances, your future plans and objectives.

Remember that any of the money invested or saved may well be taxed. This could trigger you having to pay tax, push you into a higher tax bracket or affect your entitlement to benefits.

The maximum amount should only be taken if you really need it

The more equity you release from your home, the higher the overall cost of the debt rolling up will be. If you think you may need more money at a later date, then you should look at how flexible the terms being offered are and whether you could withdraw more money as and when you require it.

Do you need to roll up the interest?

Could you or your family afford to pay it monthly so that the debt remains the same on an interest-only lifetime mortgage scheme?

Perhaps a drawdown arrangement, where you draw down money at regular intervals in smaller amounts and only take what you need as you need, it rather than a lump sum upfront, might suit you better if you are looking for income rather than an annuity bought from a lump sum. An adviser will help you when comparing and considering these options.

Interest rate options

Most schemes offer some flexibility in the interest rate options. Some are capped (that is, they will not go above an agreed level of interest), fixed for the term or they can be variable. The rate of interest will depend on the actual rates you are being charged at the time you take out the scheme. When interest rates are relatively high, the roll-up effect of your debt can build up very quickly.

With a standard variable rate, the interest repayments charged will move up or down with the lender's own mortgage rate, which is usually driven by the Bank of England's base rate. The lender may not reduce, or may delay reducing, their variable rate even if the Bank of England base rate goes down.

Fixed rates tend to be popular with borrowers who need peace of mind for the entire period of the lifetime mortgage because payments will stay the same, even if interest rates go up. This gives the security of knowing the rate at which the debt is accumulating. If rates go down, you won't benefit. Your interest rolled up will stay at the higher rate.

Should you decide to move the mortgage arrangement or pay it off early, there can be penalties, so check the terms and conditions carefully as to when any penalties may apply.

If the scheme has a 'no-negative-equity' guarantee included, that is another safeguard which ensures you cannot drop below zero equity and leave a debt for your estate when your home is eventually sold.

If the thought of the roll-up of the loan will cause you anxiety, you need to assess whether you should go ahead with such a plan and fully investigate your alternatives.

Here is an example of how the 'roll-up' effect of a mortgage will affect the amount of your debt:

£45,000 lifetime mortgage rolling up the accumulated interest			
Years since lifetime mortgage taken out	**Interest Rates**		
	5% pa	**7.5% pa**	**10% pa**
5 years	£57,433	£63,115	£69,239
10 years	£73,301	£88,522	£106,532
15 years	£93,552	£124,157	£163,912
20 years	£119,399	£174,136	£252,199
25 years	£152,387	£244,235	£388,039

Source: *Moneymadeclear* (FSA)

Looking at this example, at an interest rate of 7.5% the loan almost doubles shortly after 10 years. For the last few years we have seen relatively low interest rates but the recent economic shocks such as the 'credit crunch' in the lending market means that rates could be volatile in future. So, where a fixed rate is available against a variable rate, you will need to assess your own attitude to the risk of interest rates rising and choose accordingly. Inflation may play a part in your decision-making too. As property prices have risen, so has homeowners' 'capital wealth'.

Inheritance tax

The value of your home may now mean that you are over the Inheritance Tax (IHT) exemption (currently £300,000 per person and possibly up to £600,000 if you are widowed and your spouse's exemption has not been used). Some people consider equity release as a way to reduce their IHT liability. Releasing some money from your home could allow you to make some tax-efficient gifts during your lifetime. However, the amount of money you save in IHT may be less than the amount of interest you actually pay on the 'roll-up' mortgage.

Equity release as part of IHT planning is a very complicated area and you should seek legal and financial advice before using it.

Mr Hussein's home is worth £100,000. He borrows £30,000 at a fixed rate of interest of 6.5%. There are no monthly payments. Instead, interest is added on and rolled up over the lifetime of the loan. Because he does not pay off any interest as he goes along, the amount owed mounts up quickly. After 15 years he owes the lender £77,155. This amount includes the £30,000 he originally borrowed. When his home is sold, £77,155 must be paid to the lender. His house is now worth £200,000, so the amount of equity left which could be passed on to his family is £122,845. If his house was still only worth £100,000, the amount left that could be passed on to his family would be £22,845.

Early repayment penalties

All lifetime mortgage conditions will refer to occasions when there maybe an early repayment penalty – which is why equity release is often referred to as a 'last resort', as it is not like a normal mortgage and can be very difficult to get out of. The scheme terms and conditions will be very specific as to when a penalty may be payable.

What if you want to move house?

Everyone's circumstances change. Downsizing is sometimes not such an appealing option, as it can mean giving up a much-loved family home and moving away from family and friends. Also, the cost of downsizing could be less than that of an equity release scheme. If your partner died or had to move into long-term care, though, how would you feel about staying in your home? You might want to live somewhere nearer to a relative or move to a smaller home. If it is important that you have the option to move, then you must ensure the scheme you choose allows you the option of selling and downsizing or transferring your lifetime mortgage to a new property. All of the options ultimately will depend on your circumstances at the time, the amount of equity you have left and whether it is sufficient to meet your lender's lending criteria. Chapter 5 will cover this in more depth.

Points to check include:

- If you decide to move, can my lifetime mortgage be transferred to another property?
- What type of property is acceptable?
- What if I move to a lower-value property: can I repay part of a lifetime mortgage?
- Will I have to repay the whole of the outstanding mortgage from the proceeds of selling my property?
- If I repay the loan early, will I face early repayment charges?

Remember the amount you have to pay back could be quite high and you may end up with less than you expected for buying a new property.

Making arrangements and the costs

Taking advice is important, as you want to ensure you have covered all the things that may affect you. While, realistically, there are no complete guarantees with any advice, if you go directly to a lender then you will probably be restricted to choosing from its own options and products. Taking advice is covered in Chapter 6.

Whatever amount you release, it is important you weigh it up against the costs of setting up these types of arrangement, including such elements as the cost of advice and other options referred to in Chapter 2 that may be available to you.

The costs can be substantial and are broadly similar over a fairly wide range of property values. Typical fees and costs for arranging a lifetime mortgage are shown in this table:

Completion, arrangement or application fees	Usually £300–£600 to cover any administration costs.
Valuation fees	For a £100,000 property, £200–£300. Some companies may refund this when the loan is completed.
Solicitors' fees	Usually between £300 and £600: ask your solicitor for a breakdown of their fees. You will have to pay your own and the lender's legal costs.

Insurance	You will need buildings insurance for the period during which the plan is in place. Usually costs between £200 and £300 a year.
Your mortgage intermediary's arrangement fee	All lenders and mortgage intermediaries advising and arranging lifetime mortgages must be authorised by the FSA. If the intermediary charges a fee it must be clearly explained to you. Typically will be between 0.5% and 1.5% of the amount you are borrowing.
Early repayment charges	To cover costs in setting up the scheme, lenders may make a charge if you repay early.

Figures sourced from the Council of Mortgage Lenders and should be used as a guide only

To sum up

The lifetime mortgage market is constantly developing because of both increased competition and greater consumer awareness of the schemes and related shortcomings. More people are considering lifetime mortgages as part of their post-retirement planning. New and more flexible product options are coming onto the market and specialist 'niche' products are being developed to meet specific consumer needs, such as drawdown and the ability to take more money in the future.

This chapter has been an overview of some of the mainstream options when considering a lifetime mortgage. Further information to help you understand what your options are can be found in the useful contact addresses in Chapter 7. You will need independent financial and legal advice if you want to explore all of the aspects raised in this chapter. Make sure you are in a position to take advantage of the choices that are available and appropriate to you and that you are fully aware of the impact they will have on your finances and plans for the future.

4

Home Reversion Schemes

What is a home reversion scheme?

Home reversion schemes are another way of releasing equity from your home instead of using a lifetime mortgage. With this method you sell all or part of your home rather than mortgaging it. This method has been regulated by the Financial Service Authority (FSA) since April 2007 and means that equity release advisers must now consider the suitability for you of a home reversion plan against the option of a lifetime mortgage arrangement. Reversion schemes can, at first sight, appear more complicated than lifetime mortgages. However, they do have some benefits that lifetime mortgages do not (but can be more restrictive than lifetime mortgages regarding your future options).

It is important to note that all home reversion schemes should be regulated by the FSA – if they are not, they are illegal and do not, guarantee certain rights, such as the absolute right to continue living in your home for as long as you want or are able to do so. Unregulated schemes do not guarantee you this security – this is explained fully later in the chapter. First we will look at how these schemes work and then at what factors you need to bear in mind when considering one.

How does a home reversion scheme work?

With a home reversion scheme, you sell all or part of your home to a scheme provider in return for either a tax-free cash lump sum, a regular income or in some cases a combination of both. For example, you might sell 25% of your home and that part of it then belongs to someone else. The plan ends when you – or, if you took it out jointly, both you and your spouse or partner – die or move into permanent long-term care. The proceeds of the sale of the home are then split according to the proportion of ownership. One of the attractions of home reversion plans is that it is generally possible to raise a larger sum through them than through alternative forms of equity release.

Although the terms of the plan will vary with the provider, if you take out a reversion plan jointly with your spouse or partner and one of you dies or needs to move permanently into residential care, the plan will remain in force. This means that the remaining person can still continue to occupy the property. You sometimes pay a nominal 'rent', typically £1 each month. Certain schemes may give you a higher purchase price and in return you would pay a higher rent while you live in your home. However, you would need to be sure you would be able to continue to afford this rent payment if your circumstances change in future years.

John Green is single and 70 years old, with a mortgage-free property valued at £200,000 and no family. He is considering taking out an equity release scheme and is comparing two options available to him. First, he has been offered 25% of the value if he takes out a lifetime mortgage. This will be repaid on his death. His second option is a home reversion scheme in which he has been offered 55% of the value of the property if he transfers 100% ownership to the scheme provider.

The lifetime mortgage will provide him with a cash sum of £50,000. If this is invested in a purchased life annuity with a rate of 4% he will receive £2,000 per annum. The home reversion plan will provide him with a cash sum of £110,000 which at the same annuity rate will provide an income of £5,500 per annum. This may be the deciding factor between the two products once he has considered all other factors. It is worth noting, however, that John would be transferring 100% of the ownership of his home to the scheme provider if he chose home reversion, which means there wouldn't be anything left on the sale of the house after he dies. This isn't a problem in itself but you should be aware of it.

Unlike the case with a lifetime mortgage, there is an element of certainty as to how much money will be left in your estate. You know what percentage share of the home you have kept – you don't have to transfer 100% as John did in the example above. This means that you are able to have a rough idea of how much that share is worth (bearing in mind that property prices may fall as well as rise). Both you and the reversion scheme company will share in any increase in your property's value unless you have sold 100% of its value.

Is a home reversion scheme right for you?

A home reversion can be a useful way of releasing equity from your home but you must be sure that it is right for you.

Home reversions are usually best suited to people aged over 70. If you do not need anyone else to benefit from the full value of your home and want a lump sum or income now (and to be able to stay in your home), a home reversion may be worth considering. However, you should consider how you would feel about no longer owning your entire home. You will still have to maintain the property while you live in it at your expense and you will need to set aside money to do this. The terms of the lease and the need to make regular rent payments are also something to take into account. These factors may lead you to decide that a reversion scheme is not for you.

How much money can you release?

You will usually get between 35% and 60% of the market value of your home, depending on your age and sex, although this will vary between scheme providers. This is because the buyer is allowing you to carry on living there and cannot sell it until you either die or move into care – they may have a long wait before getting their money back. The older you are when you start the scheme, the higher the percentage value of the property you're likely to get. The percentage of the value you receive is also influenced by your state of health, the property's structure, condition and location. It is very important to shop around for individual quotes, as published percentages (such as those shown overleaf) are only a guide.

Peter Edwards is a 65-year-old man who wants to take out a home reversion scheme. His home is worth £300,000 and he sells 50% of it to the scheme provider. Although 50% of his home's value is £150,000, the provider gives him 30% of this for their share (£45,000) which he can receive as a lump sum or in regular instalments.

The scheme provider now owns 50% of his home so, if Peter died 10 years later and the property had risen in value from £300,000 to £500,000, the scheme provider would reclaim 50% of the sale price (£250,000) when the property was sold. Peter's estate (and ultimately his beneficiaries) would also receive £250,000 (for the 50% share that was retained).

Age	Typical maximum % cash available	Amount given on a property worth £200,000
65	30%	£60,000
70	38%	£76,000
75	44%	£88,000
80	50%	£100,000
85	54%	£108,000

Please note that these figures are intended as a guide only and individual providers have their own criteria.

Are home reversion schemes available to everyone?

The 'target market' for home reversion plans is broadly similar to the market for lifetime mortgages. They are aimed at people who need either to raise a cash sum or to generate an income in retirement, or a combination of the two.

Generally, home reversion plans are specifically designed for older people. However, some reversion providers make their plans available to those over 50 years of age and others restrict entry to those over a higher age. The maximum percentage of the value of the property that will be provided varies directly with age and health, so the older you are, the more you will be offered.

Home reversion schemes are not available to everyone, as certain criteria will need to be met before a provider will consider you for this type of arrangement. These include:

- your age (or age(s) if you are applying as a couple)
- the type and value of your property
- the structure and condition of the property
- who else (if anyone) lives in your home
- the state of your health.

Your age

Your age will affect your eligibility for a scheme, with all providers setting a minimum required age. If a couple are applying, then the minimum age is considered in relation to the younger applicant. Providers also tend to lend a lower percentage to couples because of the greater spread of risk to them that one of the couple will continue to occupy the home for longer.

The type and value of your property

There are minimum values that apply. These vary from scheme to scheme but are likely to be around £80,000–£100,000. Some lenders will not consider certain types of property, for example, many lenders will not lend against high-rise flats or flats above shops. Sheltered housing or types of property where you own only part of your housing are not always suitable either, nor are chalet-type 'park homes'. Some former local authority housing, for example, may not be acceptable either because the lender might be concerned that the property may not grow sufficiently in value over the time of the mortgage.

These restrictions are broadly the same as for lifetime mortgages considered in Chapter 3.

The reversion company will get a surveyor to value the property but make sure you obtain an independent valuation of your property too.

The structure and condition of the property

As with any situation where ownership of a property is being taken, the structure and condition of the property are very important as they will help to decide the value and therefore the amount you will be able to borrow. As with lifetime mortgages (see Chapter 3), the condition of the property will also be something the provider will consider in relation to your obligation to maintain the property.

The exact requirements will vary from scheme to scheme as to what your ongoing commitments will be to keep and maintain the property in a good state of repair. This is an important consideration, as maintenance costs on some older properties could be costly over the years. If you retained full ownership of the property then the decision as to how much, if any, maintenance you wanted to do would be entirely yours. Provided your lack of maintenance didn't damage your neighbour's property or cause a potential hazard to others, you could decide not to spend any money on costly repairs.

However, if you enter into a home reversion plan, then the provider of the plan will also have an interest in the property and they will want to protect their investment. Therefore there will be terms in the contract which will require you to carry out routine maintenance. The plan provider will also include terms in specifying the level of insurance you must have. They may also want to inspect your property from time to time to ensure it is in good order. Here, too, your solicitor should explain these conditions to you fully before you enter into any scheme. Other costs remaining your responsible will be bills such as council tax and utilities.

Who else lives in your home?

The property should not still have a mortgage on it or have anyone else apart from the applicant(s) living there. If someone else does live there, the lender will ask them to sign a disclaimer to say that they will give up any rights of ownership or occupation. This is to ensure that the lender can get vacant possession of the property when they need to sell it at the end of the arrangement. If you do have someone else living with you who is not going to be a party to the home reversion plan, then it is very important that both you and they understand how their rights will be affected. Your solicitor will be able to advise you about this. They will almost certainly suggest that any third party takes independent advice about their rights before signing any disclaimer (see Chapters 5 and 6).

The state of your health

Your health also influences the amount you might be able to raise; with some scheme providers offering enhanced rates if you are in poor health. An obvious concern is that you might die within a relatively short time of taking out the plan. This would make the arrangement appear to be very poor value. Sometimes protection is offered on the income element of a scheme should you die soon after taking out a plan. This gives families a rebate if you die within the first few years. It gives an agreed amount of return of capital. These types of safeguards should be looked into before you sign up for a particular scheme. Your financial adviser will be able to tell you which providers offer this option and what the costs would be.

Example of how gender and age affect the amount of cash available for a 75% share of a property worth £200,000				
Single person				
Age	Female	%	Male	%
70	£67,500	45	£73,500	49
75	£73,500	49	£79,500	53
80	£82,500	55	£87,000	58
Couple				
Age				%
Both 70		£60,000		40
Both 75		£69,000		46
Both 80		£76,500		51

Figures for illustrative purposes only

What benefits do home reversion schemes give?

- You can benefit from any possible increase in value of the property, depending on what percentage of it you still own

- There are usually no monthly repayments to make, apart from a nominal rent in some cases

- Reversion plans can sometimes be offered to younger ages (typically 55 plus) and you may be able to raise more money from your home at a younger age with a reversion plan than a lifetime mortgage would allow.

Typically, the older you are the more money you will be able to release with a reversion plan and you may be able to take further advances, depending on the amount you originally took. You should bear in mind your future needs when looking at the scheme and how your needs are likely to change in the future (see Chapter 5).

Drawbacks to home reversion schemes

- You are unlikely to receive the full market value of the share of the property you sell. This is because the reversion company will give you the absolute right to live in it, often rent free, for the rest of your life, and will not get their money back in many cases for a number of years. They therefore take this into consideration when putting a value on the share of the property they are buying. This is usually referred to as the 'discount'. For example, a 65-year-old is likely to have to give up the whole of the eventual sale proceeds of the property, in return for only 25% of its value now

- The reversion plan company owns a share of your home and will also benefit from any increases in its value and any improvements you make. There are some schemes now that offer 'limits' on this

- Reversion plans cannot usually be reversed as you are selling part of your home. So it will not be possible to change your mind at a later date if your circumstances change

- Not all reversion plan providers guarantee that they will give you a further advance should you need one. But some will allow you to move and transfer your plan, subject to meeting their criteria at that time

- If you're considering equity release because you're desperate for money now, it may not be the answer – it takes some time to arrange a scheme and it's vital to enter it with your eyes open. If you need money urgently, you should go to an advice agency for a benefits check to see whether you are claiming everything to which you are entitled. If you need the money for repaying debts, seek advice from a debt counselling service, as equity release is rarely the appropriate route. You can find details of how to contact these agencies in Chapter 7.

How should you take your money?

It may be that what you are looking for is a boost to your income rather than a lump sum. Some schemes offer a regular income in return for the sale of part of your property. This income is paid for life and it will form part of your taxable income. So, when considering how much income you will receive it is important to take into account any additional tax that might need to be paid. It could push you over your personal tax exemption level and result in you paying tax for the first time or it could mean you move into the next tax bracket and have to pay an additional tax bill. It could also affect your entitlement to benefits.

Joan Fenton is 63 years old, a non-taxpayer and has no savings. She takes a home reversion scheme income of around £500 a month, giving her an additional £6,000 a year. Part of this payment (from an annuity) is seen to be the return of her own capital but the balance of around £400 each month will form part of her taxable income. This takes her total taxable income up to £9,000 and turns her into a basic-rate taxpayer – it could also affect her entitlement to any means-tested benefits she should be claiming too.

Provided the property is your main residence, any capital released is currently tax free. However, if you invest all or part of the cash sum, the interest or investment return generated may be taxable, depending on the type of investment you use. Income produced by an annuity is split between the 'capital' element (this is the part return of your capital you invested over your lifetime) and the 'interest' element. Only the interest element is taxable.

Beware of releasing money so you can put it into an investment. An independent adviser would be able to assess whether investing your capital is a suitable thing for you to do in your particular circumstances. Remember that any investment can go down in value as well as up.

Income Tax Allowances 2008–09	
	(£)
Personal Allowance	6,035
Personal Allowance for people aged 65–74 (1)	9,030
Personal Allowance for people aged 75 and over (1)	9,180
Married Couple's Allowance (born before 6 April 1935 but aged under 75) (1), (2)	6,535
Married Couple's Allowance (aged 75 and over) (1), (2)	6,625
Income limit for age-related allowances	21,800
Minimum amount of Married Couple's Allowance	2,540
Blind Person's Allowance	1,800

(1) These allowances reduce where the income is above the income limit by £1 for every £2 of income above the limit. They will never be less than the basic Personal Allowance or minimum amount of Married Couple's Allowance.

(2) Tax relief for the Married Couple's Allowance is given at the rate of 10%.

Source: HMRC

Schemes offering a lump sum and an income

Sometimes it is possible that a scheme will advance both a lump sum and an income. Where this option is available it will usually mean you receive a smaller income. The lump sum part of this arrangement will be tax free.

Remember that the decision to take capital, income or a combination of both will have an impact on both your entitlement to benefits and your tax position. It is important you take advice to ensure that all your individual circumstances are taken into account and you have the best arrangement for you.

What if you want to move house?

This depends on the scheme you choose, although most schemes will allow you to do so – SHIP members make this a part of their Code of Practice. But it may not be so straightforward. The new property must be one which is acceptable to

65

the scheme provider (see 'The Structure and condition of the property' above). Sheltered housing is not always considered to be suitable and this option may be one that you might be considering in the future as an alternative to either coping in your home or going into residential care.

In these cases, or where the scheme can't be transferred for any reason, the only option (unless you can get the funds from elsewhere, such as your family) would be to sell the property and give the reversion company its share of the proceeds. This will limit the amount you have left to buy another property (see Chapter 5).

Making arrangements and the costs

Taking advice is important, to ensure that you take out the scheme that is best for you. If you go directly to a reversion provider you will often be restricted to the company's own products. You can find out more about the advice you should receive in Chapter 6.

Whatever amount you choose to release, it is important that it is weighed up against the costs of setting up this type of arrangement compared with the other options referred to in Chapter 2. There are substantial costs involved and these can easily add up to hundreds of pounds.

Arrangement costs

- You will have to pay an arrangement fee for setting up the scheme

- There will be legal fees and valuation fees (valuation fees are sometimes reimbursed and a contribution made towards legal fees)
- You may also have to pay a broker fee if applicable.

The reversion company will get a surveyor to value the property but make sure that you obtain an independent valuation of your property too.

Arrangement fees can be in the region of 1% to 2.5% of the amount released, depending on the scheme. If the particular scheme you are considering does not charge an arrangement fee, check how your financial adviser will be paid for their advice – see Chapter 5.

Ongoing costs

We have already identified earlier in the chapter that there may be significant costs ahead, as you will be required to maintain the property to the standard required by the reversion provider and it will reserve the right to inspect the property.

There will also be the cost of buildings insurance to insure the actual property itself. This will be a mandatory condition of taking out the plan (as it is with lifetime mortgages). Although the provider may offer you its own insurance, it is advisable to shop around. You will, however, have to have a policy which is acceptable to the provider. It may also charge to cover the administration costs of checking that the insurance policy you have taken out is acceptable.

In addition, in order to safeguard your right to stay in your home, under the lease agreement you may be required to pay a small ('peppercorn') rent – usually around £12 a year. Your solicitor will check the terms of the arrangement and explain it to you (see below).

Legal aspects

Home reversions are more complicated than lifetime mortgages and you do need independent legal advice to ensure that you understand all of the implications and that your interests are protected. You need to be sure the scheme can accommodate your future plans, as you cannot change your mind once you have signed the agreement.

In addition to doing the actual conveyancing, your solicitor will also check the agreement and explain the terms and conditions of the lease to you.

The lease will set down:

- the rights of each party
- the obligations of each party – the lease between the homeowner and the home reversion provider is open-ended and creates a right for the person(s) taking out the plan to live in the property until one of the following events occurs:
  - if a sole tenant, on their death
  - if joint tenants, on the death of the second (or last) tenant

- if a sole tenant, when they go into permanent residential care with no reasonable prospect of returning to the property

- if the last surviving tenant goes into permanent residential care with no reasonable prospect of returning to the property

- if there is any material breach of the conditions of the lease by the tenant. This will only be used as a last resort, for example where the purchaser wilfully neglects the property and by doing so causes it to fall into serious disrepair. This term is put into the contract to protect the plan provider's ownership (in whole or part) of the property.

The reversion provider may have a panel of solicitors who work in this area and can advise you. However, you have a right to use your own legal adviser and should never feel pressurised to use one suggested by the plan provider. Do not be persuaded by the suggestion that this will speed up the process. A home reversion plan is a long-term and important arrangement and you should feel absolutely comfortable with the solicitor handling the legal arrangements. However, it is true to say that equity release is a specialist area and so you should ensure that the solicitor or licensed conveyancer you use is familiar with the system. When selecting a solicitor, don't be afraid to ask them how much experience they have in this area and for a quotation for the work. (What sort of advice you can expect from your solicitor is covered in more detail in Chapter 6 'Legal and financial advice). The right to independent legal advice forms part of the SHIP Code of Practice.

Unregulated schemes

There are many different companies offering home reversion plans. Remember, they must all be regulated and this provides you with some important safeguards. Always make sure the scheme you choose is one regulated by the Financial Services Authority (FSA). The FSA contact details can be found in Chapter 7.

There are some schemes on the market that may appear at first sight to be home reversion plans but on closer inspection they are not and therefore do not need to be regulated. Sometimes these schemes are advertised and marketed as an alternative to a 'traditional' home reversion plan. It is very important to be able to recognise the difference, as these schemes will be unregulated and you will lose the valuable protection that regulation offers to you both in relation to the plan itself and to the advice you are offered.

An example of a kind of scheme that is marketed as a way of releasing equity from your home but is not a regulated scheme is 'sale and rent back'. The number of companies offering these schemes is growing and they tend to advertise heavily and be marketed as an alternative to a 'traditional' home reversion plan. These companies offer to purchase homes at below market value (typically 70%–80%) and rent them back to the former owners but without the security of a regulated home reversion scheme. The companies may offer to meet all the upfront arrangement fees and legal costs and to complete the transaction very quickly.

This means you will have access to the funds at no cost to yourself and within a relatively short space of time, which at first may appear to be very attractive. Some companies even offer to sell the property back at the current market value at a later date.

Although these schemes are marketed as being a low-cost and speedy option, there are some important disadvantages to them when compared with regulated home reversion plans.

Key areas of concern

The two key areas where you will have much less protection than with a home reversion plan are in relation to security of tenure (the right to stay in your home) and the rent that is charged to do so. Things like service charges and maintenance costs could also be out of your control.

You will usually be given an assured tenancy. These are the tenancy agreements used in the traditional letting market and they are intended to give rights to both a landlord and a tenant (such as the right to occupy for a specified length of time). Although you may be told this could be a specific period that can be extended, you have no legal right to insist on staying.

The company, as your landlord, can serve a 'notice to quit' at the end of the period specified in the tenancy agreement. Provided that it complies with the legal requirements of serving the right notices within the right time limits, they will be able to obtain vacant possession and you will have to leave. With these arrangements you are also vulnerable if the company which owns your property goes into liquidation. Your home will be regarded as an asset which could be sold to pay its creditors – this could result in you being evicted.

The amount of rent charged will be in the tenancy agreement but the landlord has the right under an assured shorthold tenancy to increase the rent at the end of the time stated in the agreement, provided it serves the correct notices. This means your rent could be substantially increased and be a lot more than you anticipated.

Age Concern does *not* recommend you take out an unregulated scheme. If you are considering this type of arrangement, then it is vitally important you get independent financial advice so you can compare alternatives such as a home reversion plan. It is also essential that you get independent legal advice so you are absolutely clear as to your rights. You should certainly not be rushed into taking out any plan.

Always ask whether the plan you are being offered is regulated and make sure you are given a clear 'yes' or 'no' answer. There is nothing in between! If you need cash urgently, visit an advice centre to see whether you are entitled to any financial help.

To sum up

Home reversion schemes, in the main, tend to represent a better proposition than they did in the past. The increased flexibility and the added protections that regulation has brought should make these schemes become more competitive and better value over time. This chapter has been an overview of some of the options and considerations and further sources of help can be found in Chapter 7.

You will need independent financial and legal advice if you want to be sure that you are in a position to take advantage of the best options that are available and appropriate to you. This is an important financial decision and the emotional aspects, as well as the practical ongoing commitments of selling all or part of your home to a reversion provider, need proper consideration before you go ahead.

5

Looking Ahead

Historically, equity release plans were often only entered into as a last resort. This meant that either the applicant was very elderly at the time the plan was taken out or the decision was perhaps made on a consideration of the short-term benefits rather than the longer-term implications. With equity release now being offered to younger applicants and its potential uses becoming more widely known, more people are now considering it as an option at a much earlier stage in their financial planning. It is therefore increasingly important that the long-term implications of equity release are specifically taken into account. This chapter looks at the issues that might affect you in the long term and which you should bear in mind when deciding whether to go ahead with an equity release plan. It will highlight the issues you should be discussing with a legal adviser when deciding if equity release is right for you.

Some particular areas to consider are:

- What will be the impact on any care provision and funding I may need in the future?
- Will equity release have an effect on my options to move to another area or a smaller home in the future?

- What happens if my spouse or partner dies and my financial circumstances change?
- Would I be able to retire abroad?
- Will equity release have any effect on how I plan for Inheritance Tax?

All independent financial advisers will consider not just your immediate circumstances but also these long-term implications as part of their regulatory requirement to give best advice.

Age Concern always recommends that you take independent financial advice and also use a regulated plan or provider when raising money from your home but recognises that you do not have to do so.

Care needs

Although people are now living longer, it is not necessarily the case that these extra years are going to be ones spent in good health. You should always consider the financial impact of needing to pay for some kind of care and support as you get older – how, if at all, will equity release impact upon your options and choices?

Life expectancy at age 65 in the UK has reached its highest level ever for both men and women as the figure overleaf shows. Men aged 65 could expect to live a further 16.9 years and women a further 19.7 years.

For some people the cost of care happens suddenly, following illness, such as a serious stroke. This leads to in a relatively high level of dependency and need for help with everyday

Life expectancy at age 65 in the UK

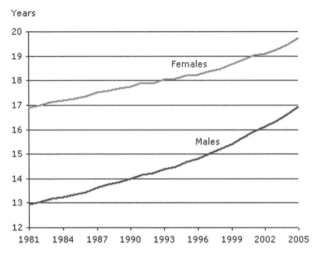

Source : National Statistics Online 2008

living. It could mean you require someone to come into your home every morning and evening and help you with shopping, meals or housework. If you don't have a live-in partner or a close friend or relative who is able to help it will usually mean having to either pay for a carer to come into your home (referred to as 'domiciliary care') or moving into a residential home.

Many people are reluctant to consider this happening to them and consequently don't budget for such expenses in their later lives. Even if they are right (and statistics show that relatively few older peope are in residential care), it would be unwise not to consider that old age can bring with it the need for additional costs for care. These usually happen gradually as you begin to need extra help, perhaps with the garden or shopping and cleaning. It may be that you want to stay in your home but it would need to be adapted in order to make it a suitable place to live if you become less mobile.

Funding for care at home

Domiciliary care may be either provided free of charge or subsidised by your local authority. Eligibility is determined by a means test of both your income and capital. If you have released a capital sum, and still have some of it available for use at the time you need domiciliary care, this may mean that you aren't eligible for free care or that you have to make a financial contribution towards the cost. Similarly, any income produced by a plan will be taken into account and may mean that you have to make a financial contribution to the cost of your care.

If you were already over the limit for local authority help with domiciliary care then the additional capital or income generated by the plan may help you to be able to fund the kind of care you need from a private provider – this would increase your options and choice.

If you are living with a spouse or civil partner, the means test only applies to the income and/or the assets held in the name of the applicant for care. If you have jointly held assets (for example, a joint bank account or building society account), then the local authority will assess half of the value of the asset as counting towards your means-test assessment.

Mr and Mrs Wilson have a joint building society account valued at £30,000. If Mrs Wilson needs domiciliary care and her local authority assesses her capital to see whether she will receive any financial help with the cost of this care, it should take into account £15,000 of the money in their joint building society account. Mr Smith's share of the account should not be taken into account.

Although local authorities have discretion about charges for care at home and their own criteria for assessment, the means-test system is national (£22,250) capital limit currently in England and Wales). The system is different in Scotland. One of these is that the value of the home is disregarded when local authorities assess the finances of people who need domiciliary care. This is the same whether the house is owned in the sole name of the applicant for care or jointly with their spouse or civil partner. However, any money taken from the home, such as by taking out an equity release plan, would count towards the means test and so could affect your entitlement to local authority funding.

Adapting the home

If you want to stay in your own home, equity release may be a good way of raising the finance to make the necessary adaptations to enable you to do so. When considering this as an option an independent adviser should always first check whether there are any grants or loans available to you, such as disabled facilities grants (see Chapter 2).

If you are thinking of taking out a plan and you currently don't need to make these adaptations, bear in mind that if you do need to do so at a later stage that any income or funds you have raised and to which you still have access (in other words, if you haven't spent the capital you have released or any income you are receiving) might affect your eligibility to any grants or loans that are means tested.

Having a carer live with you

It may be that you have discussed the possibility of needing care with your family and that there is a family member who would be willing to come and live with you and help to look after you should you need it in the future. If this is a possibility, then it must be kept in mind when deciding which equity release scheme to take as the provider will require the property to be vacant when the plan comes to an end (on death or moving into residential care).

Sheltered housing

This term is used to describe a development built especially for older people who want to be independent but who also need some additional support. Residents have their own accommodation but also have communal facilities where they can meet each other and organised activities can take place. There may be a live-in warden who helps the residents when necessary or the development may provide access to a 24-hour call telephone support service. People who have a limited need for care and support and who don't want to go into residential care frequently choose this form of care support.

Some providers of equity release plans do not consider this type of property to be suitable as security for a lifetime mortgage or as a property in which they would take shared equity (a home reversion plan). This means that if you take out a plan with this restriction and later want to move into sheltered housing, you will have to end the plan you have taken out and repay the loan – and, in the case of a lifetime mortgage, any outstanding ('rolled-up') interest. This may leave you with a limited amount of money to fund the move.

If you think that sheltered housing is an option you might consider in the future, it is important to ensure your equity release provider will allow the plan to be moved to this kind of accommodation.

Entering a care home

If you choose to go into a care home, then the equity release plan will come to an end unless your spouse or civil partner is still alive and will continue to occupy the property. In this case the plan will continue. Similarly, if your partner is the one going into care, then the plan will continue and you will be able to stay in the home.

Any income or money (you still have) from the plan will be taken into account towards the means test for residential care in the same way as described for domiciliary care above – the income and/or assets of the person going into care will be taken into account (including any that arises from the equity release plan). Joint income and money will also be assessed, as for domiciliary care, with 50% of the value being counted as the assets of the applicant.

Currently, if you have below £13,000 of capital then the local authority will fund all your care home costs. If you have over £22,250 of capital then you will have to fund all your care costs yourself. Between these two amounts you will have to make a contribution to the cost. Unlike domiciliary care, the value of the home is taken into account for the means-tested financial assessment. It will be disregarded in some situations, the most important one being if your spouse or civil partner continues to live in the home when you enter care.

If you are the only person who took out the equity release plan, then going into a care home will mean that the property will have to be sold and either the loan plus any interest repaid or, with a home reversion plan the proportion of the value of the property paid over to the reversion company. This will mean that there will be a more limited amount of money available to fund your care than if you had not entered into the plan. Any income you were receiving will cease to be paid (unless you have used a plan where the capital released has been invested in an annuity, in which case the income will continue and form part of your financial assessment). Once the final figures are worked out at the end of the plan, the amount you have left might mean that you now come within the local authority funding levels (see above) and therefore result in your care being funded by the local authority.

Moving in with relatives

It may be that you and your family have discussed your possible long-term care needs and you have all decided that you moving in with them is the right solution should the need arise. If so, the usual situation is that your home will be sold and the plan you have will come to an end. The equity left after repaying either the lifetime mortgage or the percentage share of the home reversion plan will then be available to you to invest. You will not be able to use the option of keeping your home and renting it out, as you are required to occupy the property as part of the terms and conditions of entering into these plans.

Remember: nobody can know for certain how much, if any, care they will need, so it is important to weigh the considerations above against the benefit of the immediate use of the money released by the plan, as well as whether taking the income or capital now will achieve your objectives. Access to good financial advice is very important, as an experienced independent adviser will be able to help you weigh up these considerations and decide what is right for you.

Downsizing

The possibility you might want, or need, to move to a smaller property in the future is something you should take into account when deciding if equity release is right for you. In Chapter 2 we looked at downsizing as an alternative to equity release. If downsizing isn't the right option for you right now, you still need to consider whether it might become necessary in the future. Your home might simply become too big to maintain, particularly if your partner dies and you are alone. It could be that your financial circumstances change and your home becomes to expensive too run.

If you think you might want to move to a property which is smaller and more economical to maintain in the future, you should ensure that the plan you take out will allow you to do this. Most equity release plans *will* allow you to move the scheme to a different property. Indeed, SHIP members have this as part of their Code of Practice. However, with a lifetime mortgage, if the house you are moving to is lower in value than your current home you will usually have to repay part of the mortgage.

Remember: if you cannot transfer the scheme for any reason, perhaps because the property you plan to move to is not considered suitable by your provider, you will have to repay the whole mortgage, including the rolled-up interest, from the proceeds of selling your home. The amount that you have left may not be enough to buy the kind of property that you want.

Similarly, with a home reversion plan you will usually be able to transfer the scheme but if you are unable to do so (for example because the new property is not considered to be suitable), then you will have to repay the full value of the proportion of your home you have sold.

If you think downsizing might be something you would consider in the future and you are looking to take out a home reversion plan, find out in advance what the reversion company's attitude would be to this. Ensure you have this in writing and that both parties are clear as to who would pay the costs involved. The reversion companies will have different ways of dealing with this situation; SHIP members in particular are required under their Code of Practice to ensure their plans are 'portable'.

Remember you will be vulnerable if you don't clarify this and you want to move to a smaller property, as you have sold your home to the company and if you move out the arrangement of a lease for life will come to an end.

Depending on your current financial circumstances, you might not have enough money to buy a new home. This will be particularly true if you have sold 100% of your home's value to the company – you might have to stay in your current home even though it is no longer suitable for you.

Death of a partner

If you are entering into a joint plan, it is important to consider what will happen when one of you dies before the other. The death of a spouse or partner will sometimes be the trigger for moving home either to somewhere smaller and more economical or to be nearer your family. This will be entirely your choice, as any plan taken out jointly will continue even if one of the parties to the contract dies. Your provider will not put any pressure on you to move. If the plan was taken out only in the name of the person who had died then the plan will come to an end and you will not be able to continue to live in the home. This consequence would not be unexpected, as you would both have been made aware of this limitation at the time that the plan was entered into by your partner. You would have been asked to sign a disclaimer to say that in the event of the death of the plan-holder you would give the provider vacant possession of the property. Your solicitor would also have explained this to you as part of the conveyancing process.

If you are considering taking out a home reversion plan which requires that you pay rent, be sure to consider whether the surviving partner could afford to do so if they were to be left with a reduced income. This is particularly true if you are considering paying a higher rent in return for the release of a larger amount of capital. This may seem affordable now but could be more difficult if the household income is substantially reduced.

Marriage or cohabitation

With people living longer, more people are entering into long-term relationships later in life. If you are the only one in the relationship with the equity release plan on the home you now intend to occupy as a couple, remember you need to let the plan provider know of the change in your circumstances. It will want the cohabiting partner to sign a disclaimer agreeing to give vacant possession when the plan comes to an end and ensure that everybody involved understands the situation.

It may be that your provider will allow the new partner to become a party to the plan. Ask your adviser to find out what the provider's view would be, as this will vary between companies. It is worth remembering when making a will you may not be able to put in a clause allowing your spouse or partner to continue living at your property during their lifetime after you die. If the plan is in your sole name, the plan would come to an end and any term to the contrary in the will would be ineffective. Obviously, this would not be the case if there were sufficient funds available elsewhere in your estate either to pay off the loan or to purchase the home reversion part of the property at an agreed open market value.

Moving abroad

If you think you might want to live abroad in later years, bear in mind that equity release plans are not designed to be transferred to overseas properties. This includes Guernsey, the Isle of Man and Eire. Check the geographical limits with your financial adviser.

Inheritance Tax (IHT) and estate planning

If you are considering equity release as part of estate planning, it is vital to make sure you take into account how much the equity release scheme will cost (both set-up charges and either the 'roll-up' interest for a lifetime mortgage or loss of capital value with a home reversion plan) compared with the estimated IHT saving you will make.

Currently, any estate in excess of £312,000 is taxable at the rate of 40%. As of October 2007 the IHT exemption can be more than this. Where one party to a marriage or civil partnership dies and does not use their nil rate band, the unused amount can be transferred and used by the survivor's estate on their death. This applies only where the survivor died on or after 9 October 2007.

An equity release plan could reduce your IHT bill if your estate is eligible to pay it because the mortgage (including the rolled-up interest), or the value of the share of your home sold on a home reversion plan, will have to be repaid on your death if you are the sole or surviving party to the plan. This debt will reduce the amount of your estate and consequently the amount of tax due. As explained above, this may well be an expensive option. Remember Inheritance Tax planning (sometimes referred to as 'estate planning') is a very complex matter and you should always take advice from a qualified tax adviser.

To sum up

This chapter has looked at the factors that you should take into account when considering the longer-term impact of entering into an equity release plan. All of the plans are intended to be long-term arrangements and so it is important to bear in mind the impact they might have on your long-term plans and options. An experienced, independent financial adviser will help you to weigh up the short-term benefits against any potential longer-term restrictions.

6

Legal and Financial Advice

Throughout this book we have suggested you obtain good quality, independent advice: but what does that mean? Many people do not know what to look for in an adviser and some do not want to take advice at all, preferring to use literature and websites to try to make an informed decision. In this chapter we will look at the role of both financial advisers and solicitors when you are considering whether equity release is right for you and if you progress to an application. We will highlight what the role of each of these advisers is and look at what you can expect from them.

Legal advice

If you decide to apply for an equity release plan, it's essential that you have a solicitor acting on your behalf. Equity release is a specialist area within conveyancing and it is important the solicitor you choose is familiar with the work required. This will help to make the process quicker and easier. If the solicitor is used to doing this kind of work, then they are likely to have a more streamlined procedure and this may well make the transaction less expensive, as most firms charge on an hourly rate. A specialist solicitor will be aware of the developments within the equity release industry and they will also have a good knowledge and understanding of equity release schemes which will enable them to explain everything to you in plain English.

What you can expect your solicitor to do?

Your solicitor cannot usually give you financial advice (unless they are authorised to do so) but will arrange all the legal requirements and advise you on the legal aspects of the plan.

Your solicitor will be responsible for carrying out the conveyancing. This is the term used to describe transferring the ownership of a house, flat or piece of land from one person to another. Your solicitor should explain to you the effect the plan will have on the value of your estate and can also advise you on updating or rewriting your will. They will be your contact with the lender's solicitor and ensure that all the paperwork is correct and your interests are protected. They will explain to you the legal consequences of the plan you are intending to enter into and make sure you understand these before proceeding to sign up to the plan.

As part of the conveyancing process your solicitor will be required to sign a certificate to confirm that you have been properly advised on your equity release plan and you understand the implications of taking out your chosen plan. No SHIP approved

equity release plan can be completed without this signed certificate from your solicitor.

Your solicitor will be required by the Law Society to give you certain pieces of information. These are contained in a client care letter which will include:

- the name and status of the person responsible for the day-to-day conduct of your case and the principal (senior person) responsible for the overall supervision
- a description of the work they are undertaking for you
- the charges you will have to pay and how they will be calculated
- who to approach if you feel there is a problem with their service.

In addition, if you are considering a home reversion plan, before you sign any documents that the reversion company sends, your solicitor will advise you on the terms of the lease you are being offered by the plan provider. This is the document that will allow you to continue to live in your home even though you have sold all or part of it to the provider.

Matters that need to be considered include:

- rent: how much this is and when it can be reviewed
- whether there are any restrictions on your use of the property (referred to as 'restrictive covenants')

- any insurance requirements, such as whether you must have the provider's insurance or can use your own. In the latter case this will usually require you have the approval of the provider who will want to ensure that its investment is adequately protected (some providers charge a fee for checking this).

Remember it is a regulatory requirement that the provider confirms that you have received legal advice before completing a home reversion plan.

Your solicitor will not comment on the suitability of the particular product or of the provider. However, they will talk to you in general terms about equity release and the effect that taking out a plan might have on matters such as the inheritance you want to leave, entitlement to benefits and the possible impact on your future care needs. They have to ensure that you understand the transaction you are entering into. Exactly what advice they will be giving will be set out in their correspondence with you. The description of the area of work they are undertaking for you is called the 'retainer'. They will explain the terms to you but will not make a recommendation.

Third parties

A solicitor may also explain the impact the scheme will have upon other parties who are not going to be signing the agreement.

> **Mrs Doe** is a widow and lives in her home with her unmarried daughter, Mary. The house is in Mrs Doe's sole name. She decides to enter into a lifetime mortgage so that she can increase her income. The provider has asked Mary to sign a disclaimer saying that she will vacate the property on the death of her mother, Mrs Doe or if Mrs Doe moves into residential care. Mrs Doe's solicitor can act for Mary and explain to her what the implications are of her signing the disclaimer.

A third party might also be involved where you are not handling the matter yourself but have appointed somebody to do this for you by using a power of attorney. Where someone acts on your behalf, with a power of attorney, they are under a legal obligation to act in your best interests. If the attorney is also a potential beneficiary of your estate – for example if you have appointed your son to be your attorney and he is also the person named in your will as a beneficiary – then he must not consider the effect the equity release plan might have on his inheritance when deciding whether or not to proceed. Your solicitor will advise him of his obligations as an attorney.

How do I choose a solicitor?

Your solicitor will play an important role throughout your equity release scheme application, so it's essential that you choose the right one. The Law Society has a list of solicitors who specialise in conveyancing. You can search its website by specialism and by region so that you can find a solicitor in your area: www.lawsociety.org.uk/ choosingandusing/findasolicitor.law

You need to look under 'Residential Conveyancing' and then the individual firm may specifically list 'equity release' as one of the areas in which it advises. When deciding which firm to use, don't be afraid to ask what experience it has of working in this area and compare prices.

Some equity release advisers and/or providers have lists of solicitors who specialise in this area. They should be independent from the firm which makes the recommendation and it will not be the firm who is acting for the provider. If there were to be any commercial relationship between them (for example if the financial adviser received commission for the referral) this would have to be disclosed, as there are strict rules for both financial advisers and solicitors which require them to make it clear if there is any financial benefit in such situations. With equity release you will always have a different solicitor from the one representing the provider.

If you already have your own solicitor, you may feel more comfortable using them. Check they have experience in this area before deciding to proceed.

Licensed conveyancers

Although we have referred to using a solicitor, it is also possible to use a licensed conveyancer. These are specialist property lawyers – people who are trained and qualified in all aspects of the law dealing with property. They are regulated by the Council for Licensed Conveyancers (see Chapter 7).

Powers of attorney

While carrying out your instructions regarding equity release, your solicitor will also check whether you have a power of attorney.

This might be an enduring power of attorney or a new lasting power of attorney. These powers of attorney allow someone you have named to make decisions for you. Enduring powers of attorney allow the named person(s) to make decisions about your property and finance. These powers were replaced by lasting powers of attorney in October 2007.

These new powers allow you to choose people to make not only financial decisions but also decisions about your health and welfare. The latter decisions can only be made if you have lost the capacity to make these decisions for yourself.

 If you already have an enduring power of attorney this will still be valid provided it was signed and witnessed on or before 30 September 2007.

More information about powers of attorney can be found on the website of the Office of the Public Guardian or in Age Concern Factsheet FS22 *Arranging for others to make decisions about your finances or welfare*.

Wills

Equity release will clearly have an impact on the inheritance that you will leave, so this is an obvious time to review your wishes. Even if you have a will, it may be some time since you last reviewed it. Your solicitor will explain the effect of the equity release plan on your estate.

If you take out a lifetime mortgage, the amount borrowed plus the 'rolled-up interest' must be re-paid by your executors before they make payments under your will to any of the beneficiaries. Your estate will therefore be reduced by this amount. If you have taken out a home reversion plan, you may have no value in your home to leave to your beneficiaries (for example if you have taken out a 100% reversion plan). If you have retained a share for yourself, then this amount will be free to pass to your beneficiaries after the value of the percentage owned by the reversion company has been paid to it.

If you already have a will, this will be a good time to review it and see if it still reflects your wishes. Your solicitor will also enquire into your personal circumstances to make sure, the will is still up to date; for example, you or your children could have got married or divorced, or one or more of the beneficiaries could have died.

Your solicitor will also explain who will inherit if you don't have a will. The law of 'intestacy' will mean that specified people will get a share. These may not be the people you would want to benefit. Finally, you will need to consider if your will is tax efficient; for example, whether it will minimise any Inheritance Tax that might be due on your death.

For more information about making a will, see Age Concern Factsheet FS7 or visit the Government website at www.direct.gov.uk/en/ RightsAndResponsibilities/Death/Preparation/DG_ 10029800

Complaints

Should you have a complaint about your solicitor that cannot be resolved through the solicitor's own complaints procedure, you can go to the Legal Complaints Service (see Chapter 7), which is part of The Law Society.

Financial advice

A key part of making sure that equity release is right for you is to ensure you only take advice from those who are well qualified to help you. Most of the equity release providers will only take instructions through a regulated intermediary; in other words, a financial adviser.

It is possible to take out a plan without any help but this means that you would have very limited options for redress if it emerged that the plan wasn't suitable – this way of taking out a plan is called 'transaction only'. But, the majority of plans are sold with advice. A good financial adviser will help you choose a suitable plan but also (and most importantly) decide whether equity release itself is the right option to take at all.

There have been problems in the past with the advice given in relation to equity release and there have been accounts of people losing their homes and being sold expensive, inflexible and unregulated schemes. However, financial advice has improved considerably and equity release is now regulated by the FSA. It has regulated the sale of lifetime mortgage products since October 2004 and the sale of home reversion plans since April 2007.

For both forms of equity release transaction, advisers must consider whether the benefits to the customer of taking out equity release outweigh any adverse effect on the customer's entitlement to means-tested benefits, and also the effect on their tax position. If you take regulated advice you have a greater degree of protection if you are sold a scheme that was not suitable for you. An authorised adviser should also look at your wider needs too and how taking equity release will affect your options later when you may need to move or go into long-term care, for example. There are factors that are not always easy to consider by yourself.

You need to ensure that any person giving you financial advice is regulated by the FSA or is the agent of a regulated firm. Regulated firms and their agents can be checked on the FSA's Register at www.fsa.gov.uk/register or by contacting the FSA on 0845 606 1234.

If you need to make a complaint, the regulated firm/person you deal with should have outlined how you can do this in the written information it provided to you. More information about making a complaint can be obtained from the FSA.

If you take an equity release product that is not from a regulated provider they are not subject to FSA regulation and you won't have access to the complaints and compensation procedures of the Financial Services Ombudsman Service and the Financial Services Compensation Scheme (see Chapter 7).

Adviser qualifications

The regulation of equity release plans extends to the sale and marketing of equity release schemes. As part of the new regulatory requirements, anyone advising you on any form of equity release must attain an 'appropriate qualification'. Don't feel awkward about asking them what their qualifications are in this area. You can see what qualifications an adviser should have by going to the SHIP website: www.ship-ltd.org/img/qual-table.pdf

Information or advice

When you ask about an equity release scheme, the person you speak to will usually describe the product or service to you and you will also receive printed literature. This is only general information and not specific advice relating to your needs and circumstances. It is important to be aware of the difference between advice and information. If you are not sure, ask: 'Is this advice you are giving me or just information?'

FSA-regulated firms must only recommend schemes that are suitable for you and take into consideration your needs and circumstances. In all advised equity release sales, advisers will be required to consider alternative equity release options – so, for example, lifetime mortgage sales processes must include a general consideration of whether you would be better off with a home reversion plan and vice versa. An adviser will need good generic knowledge of how each product works. Make sure you fully understand the advice you are being given before you proceed.

The service offered and costs

Under FSA rules, financial advisers must give you written information about both the service they offer and how much it will cost. They must explain the type of service they offer (information or advice), whose products they choose from (the whole market, from a limited range or from just one provider) and how you're being charged for the service (fees and/or commission). A financial adviser can only say they offer independent advice if they recommend from the whole market and offer you the option to pay a fee rather than commission.

Your financial adviser must also give you documents which set out the key features of the scheme(s), including the risks and the benefits to you. This must be in a clear standard format to help you understand and compare it with other products. The FSA also requires that its advertisements, product brochures and other literature must be comprehensive, fair and not misleading.

The advice you receive is not free and either you will pay a fee to the firm or a commission fee will be paid to the adviser from the product provider. If commission is paid, it may feel as though you have got free advice but the money will come from the sum you raise on your property. It will be shown as one of the costs of the arrangement.

Independent financial advisers work on your behalf rather than on behalf of a product provider. If you use an independent financial adviser, you will also be able to choose how you pay for your advice as they must offer you the option of paying a fee or a commission. Make sure you are clear about the costs, as equity release involves other fees in addition to those for advice. If you are looking to raise a small amount of capital, you need to weigh up all the costs involved to make sure it is financially worthwhile.

Remember to check whether the adviser is recommending products from the whole of the market or whether they are only able to offer products from one company or a limited range of companies.

Questions to ask your financial adviser

Here are some of the questions you might like to ask:

- Are you an independent equity release adviser or tied to a provider of products and services?
- What are your qualifications?
- Is equity release my best option, considering my personal financial circumstances?

- Are there any benefits I may be entitled to that I either don't currently get or may lose if I take out an equity release scheme?

- How will taking out an equity release scheme affect my options in the future when it comes to moving home if, say, my partner dies or if I need to fund my own long-term care?

- What is the 'real cost' of the scheme? If, for example, I am making an investment into an annuity to boost my income, how will inflation affect things?

- What about the different types of schemes – why might I be better off with one than another?

- What about protection – am I covered under the SHIP scheme and under the various Financial Services Compensation Scheme terms if I need to complain?

- What are your fees and how do I pay for the advice and the costs to set up the scheme?

- What about the family – how might this affect my spouse and what will be the effect of the plan on any inheritance I want to leave my family?

Having read this book, you should be well prepared to deal with an adviser and to pick one who can meet your needs. These are important decisions you are considering, so investigate your options fully. It is useful to ask friends for any recommendations they may have or any suggestions as to who to avoid! Do not rush into a quick decision. Many independent financial advisers will agree to a free initial 'no obligation' meeting. You may have to see more than one before you find a person you are comfortable with and feel you can trust. Remember that you are dealing with what's likely to be your most valuable financial asset.

7

More Help

Pensions, benefits and tax

Department for Work and Pensions (DWP)
Tel: 0800 88 22 00 (benefit enquiry line)
www.dwp.gov.uk
Confidential advice and information for people with disabilities, and their carers and professional advisers. Social security benefits and how to claim them.

The Pension Service
Tel: 0845 6065 065
www.thepensionservice.gov.uk
For information about pensions and pensioner benefits, for those planning for the future, about to retire or already retired.

HM Revenue & Customs
www.hmrc.gov.uk
HMRC is responsible for collecting the bulk of tax revenue, as well as paying Tax Credits and Child Benefits.

Consumer Credit Counselling Service
Wade House
Merrion Centre
Leeds LS2 8NG
Tel: 08001381111
www.cccs.co.uk
CCCS is a registered charity offering free, confidential advice and support to anyone who is worried about debt. A free counselling and debt advice can help you get back in control of your money.

Disability Alliance
Universal House
88–94 Wentworth Street
London E1 7SA
Tel: 020 7247 8776
www.disabilityalliance.org
Information on social security benefits and tax credits to disabled people, their families, carers and professional advisers; particular emphasis on income needs and promote a wider understanding of the views and circumstances of all disabled people.

Warm Front
eaga House
Archbold Terrace, Jesmond
Newcastle Upon Tyne NE2 1DB
Tel: 0800 316 2805 (to apply for a grant)
Tel: 0800 072 9006 (to check if you qualify)

Tel: 0800 316 6011 (customer services)
www.warmfront.co.uk
Warm Front makes homes warmer, healthier and more energy-efficient. It is a Government-funded initiative and the scheme is managed by eaga. If you own your own home or rent it from a private landlord, you may be eligible for a grant under the Warm Front Scheme.

Financial advice

Financial Services Authority
25 The North Colonnade,
Canary Wharf,
London E14 5HS
Tel: 0845 606 1234 (helpline)
www.fsa.gov.uk
An independent body that regulates the financial services industry in the UK. It maintains an open central register of financial advisers this can be searched via its website.

Moneymadeclear
www.moneymadeclear.fsa.gov.uk
Moneymadeclear from the FSA cuts out the jargon and give you just the facts about financial products and services, helping you to make an informed decision.

Financial Services Compensation Scheme
7th floor, Lloyds Chambers
Portsoken Street

London E1 8BN
Tel: 020 7892 7300
www.fscs.org.uk
FSCS is an independent body, set up under the Financial Services & Markets Act 2000 as the UK's compensation fund of last resort for customers of financial services firms. This means that FSCS can pay compensation to consumers if an authorised financial services firm is unable, or likely to be unable, to pay claims against it.

Association of Independent Financial Advisers. (AIFA)
2–6 Austin Friars House
Austin Friars
London EC2N 2HD
Tel: 020 7628 1287
www.aifa.net
AIFA is the voice of the IFA profession.

Association of Mortgage Intermediaries (AMI)
2–6 Austin Friars House
Austin Friars
London EC2N 2HD
Tel: 020 7628 1288
www.a-m-i.org.uk
AMI is an independent source of information – go to their website: (www.adviserlists.co.uk/equity) this gives you the opportunity to search for an IFA in your area specialising in Equity Release.

National Debtline
Tricorn House
51–53 Hagley Road,
Edgbaston

Birmingham B16 8TP
Tel: 0808 808 4000
(freephone)
www.nationaldebtline.co.uk
*National Debtline is a national
telephone helpline for people
with debt problems in
England, Wales and
Scotland; the service is free,
confidential and independent.*

Regulators

Financial Services Authority (FSA)
25 The Colonnade
Canary Wharf
London E14 9SR
Tel: 020 7676 1000
www.fsa.gov.uk
*The FSA has been given a
wide range of rule-making,
investigatory and enforcement
powers in order to meet
statutory objectives. In
meeting these they are
obliged to have regard to the
Principles of Good Regulation.*

The Financial Ombudsman Service (FOS)
South Quay Plaza
183 Marsh Wall
London E14 9SR
Tel: 0845 080 1800 or 020
7964 0500
www.financialombudsman.
org.uk
*The independent service for
settling disputes between
consumers and businesses
providing financial services*

Council for Licensed Conveyancers (CLC)
16 Glebe Road
Chelmsford
Essex CM1 1QG
Tel: 01245 349599
www.conveyancer.org.uk
*The regulatory body for
Licensed Conveyancers who
are qualified specialist
property lawyers.*

Safe Home Income Plans (SHIP)
83 Victoria Street
London SW1H 0HW
Tel: 0870 241 6060
www.ship-ltd.org
*An organisation supported by
the leading providers of home
income and equity release
plans. It was launched in
1991 and is dedicated
entirely to the protection of
those looking at equity
release plans as an option,
and promotion of safe home
income and equity release
plans.*

Solicitors Regulatory Authority (SRA)
Tel: 0870 606 2555
www.sra.org.uk
*The SRA regulates more than
100,000 solicitors in England
and Wales. Its purpose is to
protect the public by
ensuring that solicitors meet
high standards and by acting
when risks are identified.*

Housing and accommodation

Home Improvement Trust (HIT)
7 Mansfield Road
Nottingham NG1 3FB
Tel: 0800 783 7569
www.houseproud.org.uk
HIT's aim is to enable older and disabled people to live safely and independently in their own home, helping to prevent poor health and reducing the need for residential care.

Home Improvement Agencies (HIA)
Foundations
Bleaklow House
Howard Town Mill, Glossop
Derbyshire SK13 8HT
Tel: 01457 891909
www.foundations.uk.com
Home Improvement Agencies are locally based, not-for-profit organisations. They help older, disabled and vulnerable homeowners or private tenants to repair, improve, maintain or adapt their homes. HIA's prime purpose is to help people continue to live safely in their own homes in comfort, with security and independence.

Care and Repair England
The Renewal Trust Business Centre
3 Hawksworth Street
Nottingham NG3 2EG
Tel: 01159 506500
www.careandrepair-england.org.uk
Care & Repair England works to enable older and disabled people to live independent lives in their own homes for as long as they wish. They work directly with people who live in poor or inadequate housing conditions.

Care and Repair Forum Scotland
135 Buchanan Street
Suite 2.5
Glasgow G1 2JA
Tel: 0141 221 9879
www.careandrepairscotland.co.uk
Care & Repair Scotland offer independent advice and assistance to help homeowners repair, improve or adapt their homes so they can live in comfort and safety at home in their own community.

Care and Repair Cymru
Norbury House
Norbury Road, Fairwater
Cardiff CF5 3AS
Tel: 029 2057 6286
www.careandrepair.org.uk
Care & Repair Cymru is the national body that actively works to ensure all older people have homes that are safe, secure and appropriate to their needs.

Fold Housing Association
3-7 Reburn Square
Holywood
Co Down BT18 9HZ
Tel: 028 90428314

www.foldgroup.co.uk
Fold's workforce provides a range of services which allow people to live longer in their own homes or independently within a secure and supportive environment.

College of Occupational Therapists
106–114 Borough High Street
London SE1 1LB
Tel: 020 7357 6480
www.cot.org.uk
Occupational therapy takes a hands-on role with individuals or groups of clients. Their job is to equip people so they can take part in everyday activities and live more satisfying lives.

Elderly Accommodation Counsel (EAC)
3rd Floor, 89 Albert Embankment
London SE1 7TP
Tel: 020 7820 1343
www.eac.org.uk
EAC offer an advice service directly to older people their relatives and carers, they raise awareness of the importance people attach to information which helps them make their own decisions about how and where to live in older age.

Legal advice

The Law Society
The Law Society's Hall
113 Chancery Lane
London WC2A 1PL

Tel: +44 (0) 20 7242 1222
www.lawsociety.org.uk
The Law Society represents solicitors in England and Wales. Their website offers a searchable database to help find a solicitor (by firm name, postcode or area of law). They offer advice on what to expect, guides to common legal problems and what to do if things go wrong.

Law Society in Wales
Capital Tower
Greyfriars Road
Cardiff CF10 3AG
Tel: 02920 645 254
www.lawsociety.org.uk
The office represents the Society's view and interests to members of the National Assembly; they offer a bi-lingual service.

Law Society of Scotland
26 Drumsheugh Gardens
Edinburgh EH3 7YR
Tel: 0131 226 7411
www.lawscot.org.uk
The Law Society promotes the interests of the solicitors' profession in Scotland and the interests of the public in relation to the profession. There is a searchable database on the website to help with finding a solicitor.

Law Society of Northern Ireland
(Society's address while its premises in Victoria Street, Belfast, are being renewed)
40 Linenhall Street
Belfast BT2 8BA

Main address
Law Society House
98 Victoria Street
Belfast BT1 3JZ
Tel: 028 9023 1614
www.lawsoc-ni.org
The regulatory authority governing the ethical standards, professional competence and quality of services offered to the public. There is a searchable database on the website to help with finding a firm of solicitors.

Community Legal Service (CLS)

Tel: 0845 345 4 345
www.clsdirect.org.uk
CLS is a free and confidential advice service paid for by legal aid. If you live on a low income or benefits call for independent advice about debt, benefits and tax credits, employment and housing problems.

Legal Complaints Service (LCS)

Victoria Court, 8 Dormer Place
Leamington Spa
Warwickshire CV32 5AE
Tel: 0845 608 6565 (helpline)
www.legalcomplaints.org.uk
LCS investigates complaints about solicitors. They handle over 300 calls a day on a range of legal complaints.

Solicitors for the Elderly (SFE)

Room 17, Conbar House
Mead Lane, Hertford
Herts SG13 7AP
Tel: 08700670282
www.solicitorsfortheelderly.
com
SFE is a national organisation of lawyers, solicitors, barristers, and legal executives who are committed to providing and promoting robust, comprehensive and independent legal advice for older people, their family and carers.

General advice

Age Concern England

Astral House
1268 London Road
LondonSW16 4ER
Tel: 0800 00 99 66 (helpline)
www.ace.org.uk
ACE offers help, advice and support to older people, their carers and relatives. Information and factsheets relating to issues of direct concerns can be ordered or downloaded direct from the website. Age Concern publishes a wide range of best selling that help thousands of people each year; 'phone line 0870 44 22 120 for more details.

Citizens Advice Bureau (CAB)

Myddelton House
115–123 Pentonville Road
London N1 9LZ
Tel: 020 7833 2181 (admin only no advice given)
www.citizensadvice.org.uk

www.adviceguide.org.uk
The CAB service helps people resolve their housing, legal, money and other problems by providing free information and advice from 3,300 locations. There is a database on their website which helps you find your nearest CAB office.

Counsel and Care
Twyman House
16 Bonny Street
London NW1 9PG
Tel: 0845 300 7585
www.counselandcare.org.uk
A national charity provides support for older people, their families and carers. They provide advice, information and financial support. Many older people rely on the help and encouragement given by their Advice Workers to navigate the care system.

Help the Aged
207–221 Pentonville Road
London N1 9UZ
Tel: 020 7278 1114
Help the Aged is an international charity fighting to free older people from poverty, isolation and neglect. HTA have a subsidiary that offers advice on Equity Release and whether it is right for you.

Glossary

Annuity

An annuity converts a lump sum into an income which is taxed. It is a financial product purchased from an insurance company that guarantees to pay a set amount at regular intervals (normally monthly).

APR

Annual percentage rate – the APR is the best rate to use when comparing mortgage offers. It tells you:

- the interest rate you must pay
- how you repay the loan (length of loan agreement (or term), frequency and timing of instalment payments and amounts of each payment)
- certain fees associated with the loan
- certain compulsory insurance premiums (for example, payment protection insurance).

Arrangement fee

A commitment or administration fee usually payable to the provider.

Bonds

Bonds are investments that provide a set level of income. Usually they expire at the end of a fixed term, when they pay a specified amount of money. Bond payments are usually guaranteed but the strength of the guarantee depends on the organisation providing it.

Broker/intermediary

A person who will arrange a mortgage with a lender. Mortgage brokers must tell you which lenders they use and how much lenders pay them for arranging mortgages.

Buildings insurance

Insurance to cover the cost of repairing or rebuilding your home if it is damaged or destroyed.

Capital

The amount you have borrowed on the mortgage. This is the amount on which you will be charged interest and which you will have to repay at the end of the mortgage term.

Civil partnerships

Legislation has been passed to allow same-sex couples to enter into a formal partnership, called a civil partnership. Civil partners will be entitled to some of the same rights, as well as carrying some of the same responsibilities, as married couples.

Completion

When you become the legal owner of landed property.

Contract

The legal document which transfers the ownership of the property from the seller to the buyer.

Conveyancer

A solicitor or licensed conveyancer who does the legal work involved in selling and buying property.

Conveyancing

The legal work involved in selling and buying property.

Disbursements

The fees, such as Stamp Duty and Land Registry fees, which you pay to the conveyancer.

Drawdown mortgage

This is a form of lifetime mortgage where you don't withdraw the full sum of money available to you immediately. Instead, you decide on a maximum amount of equity you want to release, and 'draw down' the cash in stages.

Equity release

This term refers to ways in which you can benefit from the value of your home without having to move out. This is done by borrowing against the value of your property or by selling all or part of it in return for a regular income or a lump sum.

Estate planning

This is the term used to describe organising your assets and other investments to minimise any obligation to pay Inheritance Tax when you die. It usually also involves considerations of how to ensure that any surviving spouse or partner still has appropriate financial resources.

Financial Ombudsman

The Financial Ombudsman is an independent body set up by law to provide a free service to help consumers settle individual disputes with firms providing investment advice or services.

Financial Services Authority

The FSA is an independent body set up by the Government to regulate the financial services industry.

Financial Services Compensation Scheme

The FSCS is an arrangement set up by the Government to ensure that, if a financial services provider (for example, a bank or insurance company) becomes insolvent, its customers will have some financial compensation. The FSCS is financed by levies on the industries covered.

Fixed-repayment lifetime mortgage

You take out a loan that pays you a cash lump sum and, instead of paying any interest on the loan, you pay the lender an agreed amount which is more than you borrowed when you sold your home.

Ground rent

A yearly fee that leaseholders have to pay to the freeholder or landlord who owns the land on which the leasehold property is situated.

Home income plan

You take out a loan that pays you a cash lump sum and is secured against your home. You then buy an annuity to give you a monthly income, usually fixed for life (see 'Annuity').

Home reversion

You sell all or part of your home to a third party in return for regular income and/or a cash lump sum and continue to live in your home for as long as you wish.

Interest

The money you are charged for borrowing.

Interest-only mortgage

You take out a loan on which you only pay the interest back each month. You do not pay off any of the capital. Instead, in a lifetime mortgage, the lender will be repaid by selling your home when you die or go into long-term care.

Land Registry fee

A fee paid to the Land Registry to register ownership of a property.

Leaseholder

Someone who owns a property, but not the land it stands on, for a fixed period of time.

Lease

A legal contract which gives the ownership of a leasehold property to the buyer for a fixed period of time.

Legal fees

Fees you pay to your solicitor for their services.

Lifetime mortgage

You take out a loan secured on your home, which is repaid by selling your home when you die or go into long-term care.

Mortgage

A loan to buy a property. The property acts as security for the loan and so can be re-possessed and sold if the mortgage repayments are not made.

Mortgage application fees

These are fees charged by the lender in return for organising the mortgage for you. These are not usually refunded if you then do not go ahead with the mortgage.

Mortgage deed

The legal agreement which gives the lender a legal right to a property.

Mortgage term

The length of time over which the mortgage will be repaid.

Negative equity

This is the term used to describe the situation where the amount you owe the lender is more than the value of your home.

Offer of advance

The formal offer of a mortgage from a lender.

Powers of attorney

There may come a time when you are incapable of managing your property and financial affairs and need someone to do this for you. You can formally appoint a friend, relative or professional to make these decisions for you by giving them a power of attorney. This power comes to an end when you lose capacity. However, a particular form is an enduring power of attorney (EPA) which will continue when you lose capacity. Since October 2007 EPAs can no longer be created. Instead, you use a lasting power of attorney. These allow you to appoint somebody to make personal welfare decisions for you as well as financial ones.

Redemption
The paying off of a mortgage loan.

Retention
When the lender holds back some of the mortgage money until certain repairs have been done, the amount held back is known as a 'retention'.

Roll-up mortgage
You take out a loan as regular income or a cash lump sum. The interest on the loan is rolled up each month or year and added to the loan. This means you may end up owing more than the value of your home (in other words, more than you borrowed). This is referred to as 'negative equity' (see above).

Secured
This term is used to describe the process by which the lender ensures that they can get their money back by placing a legal 'charge' over the property. If you do not keep up the payments on your loan, the lender can then sell your home to get its money back.

Security
The property the mortgage is being used to buy is the lender's 'security' for the loan. This means that the lender has rights over the property. If the mortgage repayments are not kept up to date, the lender can repossess the property and sell it to recover the debt.

Shared appreciation mortgage

You borrow a lump sum based on the value of your home
and nothing is repaid until you die or the property is sold.
At that stage, the amount you originally borrowed is paid
back, together with an agreed percentage of the amount
by which your home has increased in value.

Stamp Duty

A government tax on buying properties costing more than
£125,000.

Index

About Age Concern

Age Concern is the UK's largest organisation working for and with older people to enable them to make more of life. We are a federation of over 400 independent charities who share the same name, values and standards and believe that later life should be fulfilling, enjoyable and productive.

Age Concern England
1268 London Road
London SW16 4ER
SW16 4ER
Tel: 020 8765 7200
www.ageconcern.org.uk

Age Concern Cymru
Ty John Pathy
Units 13 and 14 Neptune Court
Vanguard Way, Cardiff CF24 5PJ
Tel: 029 2043 1555
www.accymru.org.uk

Age Concern Scotland
Causewayside House
160 Causewayside
Edinburgh EH9 1PP
Tel: 0845 833 0200
www.ageconcernscotland.org.uk

Age Concern Northern Ireland
3 Lower Crescent
Belfast BT7 1NR
Tel: 028 9024 5729
www.ageconcernni.org

Age Concern Books

Age Concern publishes a wide range of bestselling books that help thousands of people each year. They provide practical, trusted advice on subjects ranging from pensions and planning for retirement, to using a computer and surfing the internet. Whether you are caring for someone with a health problem or want to know more about your rights to healthcare, we have something for everyone.

Ordering is easy To order any of our books or request our free catalogue simply choose one of the following options:

☎ **Call us on 0870 44 22 120**

🖱 **Visit our website at www.ageconcern.org.uk/bookshop**

✉ **Email us at sales@ageconcernbooks.co.uk**

You can also buy our books from all good bookshops.